ENGLISH INTERIORS 1790–1848

ENGLISH INTERIORS
1790–1848

The Quest For Comfort

JOHN CORNFORTH

BARRIE & JENKINS
COMMUNICA - EUROPA

In Memory of
JOHN FOWLER
who taught many friends so much

© John Cornforth 1978

First published in 1978 by
Barrie & Jenkins Ltd
24 Highbury Crescent, London N5 1RX

ISBN 0 214 20290 9

Typeset in Garamond by Jolly & Barber Ltd, Rugby, Warwickshire

Origination and printing by Jolly & Barber Ltd.

Bound by W. & J. Mackay Ltd, Chatham

Designed by John Leath, MSTD

CONTENTS

ACKNOWLEDGEMENTS

Frequently it is forgotten what a nuisance writers and researchers can be to owners, asking not easily answered questions and requesting prints from non-existent negatives or asking for permission to photograph. A book of this kind depends entirely on the co-operation of private owners and curators of public collections of many kinds, and to all those named below I would like to express my thanks.

In addition there are many people who have provided answers to questions and made helpful suggestions – too many, alas, to mention by name. Here John Harris counts not only as an owner, but as someone who has allowed me to use his books on many occasions and has discussed puzzling houses. Others who share my enthusiasm for Mario Praz's book and who have put me on to many pictures over a period of years include Guy Acloque; Desmond Fitzgerald, the Knight of Glin; Emilie Gwynne-Jones; Gervase Jackson-Stops; Merlin Waterson; John Hardy, who has kept a complementary file in the Woodwork Department of the Victoria and Albert Museum; and, of course, colleagues past and present at *Country Life*, who have had drawings photographed for country house articles on a number of occasions during the past fifty odd years.

The Editor of *Country Life* has given permission to reproduce numerous photographs; most of the recent ones have been taken by Alex Starkey. Francesca Barran has assisted me in getting National Trust pictures photographed, and most of these pictures as well as many others have been taken specially for the book by Angelo Hornak.

OWNERS

Trustees of the Chatsworth Settlement I, 2, 3, 4, 5, 6, 10, 11, 89; Mr John Harris II, 8, 12, 13, 14, 15, 16, 25, 26, 27, 28, 31, 32, 34, 58, 61, 62, 133, 134, 135, 136, 137, 140, 141, 156; Mr Nigel Stopford Sackville III; Mr F. H. Fitzroy Newdegate IV; British Museum V, 18, 19, 104, 105, 106, 107, 124, 154, 155, 156, 158, 159, 172; Mrs J. R. Ede VI; Towneley Hall Art Gallery & Museums, Burnley Borough Council VII; Lord St Oswald VIII; Museum of London IX, 108, 109; National Galleries of Scotland X; Victoria and Albert Museum XI, 1, 44, 45, 46, 47, 48, 127, 129, 166; The Duke of Buccleuch and Queensberry XII; The Marquess of Salisbury 7, 9; National Trust 17, 20, 21, 22, 23, 81, 82, 138, 139, 143, 175; Mr George Howard 24; Woburn Abbey Collection, by permission of the Marquess of Tavistock and Trustees of the Bedford Estates 29, 30; Kent County Council, Education Department, County Library, Folkestone 33; The Duke of Westminster 35, 36, 37, 103; Lord Howard de Walden 38, 39, 40, 41, 42; The Earl of Mount Edgcumbe 43; Mr T. W. Ferrers-Walker 49; The Earl of Dunraven and Mount Earl 50, 51; Ashmolean Museum, Oxford 52, 53, 54, 125, 146, 147, 148, 149, 150; Major J. R. Mather 55, 56, 57, 96, 97; Mr David J. Hoare 59; The Rev Henry Stapleton 60; Sir Richard Sykes, Bart 64, 66; Brierley, Leckenby, Keighley & Groom 65; Sir Richard Proby, Bart 67; The Duke of Wellington 68, 69; Mr Reresby Sitwell 70, 71, 72, 73, 74; Sir Walter Bromley Davenport, Bart 75, 76, 77, 78, 79, 80, 145; Mr & Mrs Paul Mellon 83; Lady Lucas 84, 85, 86; The Rev Henry Thorold 87; Mr Myles Hildyard 88; Laing Art Gallery, Newcastle upon Tyne (Tyne and Wear County Council Museums) 90; The Earl of Mansfield 91; Miss Elizabeth Johnstone 92, 93; The Earl of Normanton 94, 95; Nancy, Lady Bagot 98, 100; Mr Paul Grinke 63, 99, 164, 165; Magdalene College, Cambridge 101, 102; Royal Borough of Kensington & Chelsea, Central Library 110, 111, 112, 113, 114; Guildhall Library, London 115; Sir John Soane's Museum 116, 117, 118, 119, 120, 121, 122; Mr Paul Paget 126; Mr W. S. Lewis 128, 130, 131, 132; Mr James Lees-Milne 142; The Knight of Glin 144, 172; Cowper & Newton Museum, Olney 160; Mr Nicholas Horton Fawkes 161, 162, 163; Miss Janet Hughes 168; Abbott Hall Art Gallery 169; Mrs Meikle 171; The Trustees of the National Library of Scotland 170; Mr John Chichester-Constable 173; The Marquess of Northampton 174.

PHOTOGRAPHS

Trustees of the Chatsworth Settlement I; Angelo Hornak II, 2–6, 8, 12, 14, 16, 20, 21, 23, 25–28, 31, 32, 34, 44–48, 55–57, 58, 61, 62, 71–74, 82, 94–97, 99, 113, 114, 127, 136, 137, 140, 141, 151–157, 164, 165; National Portrait Gallery III; *Country Life* IV, VII, XII, 10, 11, 13, 15, 35–43, 49, 51–54, 59, 64, 66–70, 75–78, 89, 118, 122, 125, 126, 142, 145–150, 161–163, 173; British Museum V, 18, 19, 104–107, 124, 154, 155, 156, 157, 158, 159; Miss Lucinda Fletcher, 151, 152, 153; Victoria and Albert Museum VI, XI, 129; Jeremy Whitaker VIII; Museum of London IX, 108, 109; Annan, Glasgow X; J. R. Freeman 1; B. L. King 7, 9; Courtauld Institute 22, 81, 84–86, 103; Keith Gibson 24; Patrick Rossmore 50; Norman Jones 63; Ken Pettinger 65; National Monuments Record 79, 80; Philipson Studios 90; Tom Scott 91; Charles Woolf 92, 93; Peter Rogers 98, 100; Edward Leigh 101, 102; Kensington Library 110–112; A. C. Cooper 115; Godfrey New 116, 117, 119–121; Trevor Yorke 156; Abbott Hall Art Gallery 168–171; John Bethell 174; Rodney Todd White, 138, 139.

FOREWORD

Few books have given me as much pleasure as Mario Praz's *Illustrated History of Interior Decoration*, published in the easier climate of 1964, and every time I take it off the shelf I see in its plates details that I have not noticed before. It was particularly stimulating when I was at work with John Fowler on our book *English Decoration in the 18th Century*, and it prompted me to look out for pictures of English rooms. From those I had seen in old issues of *Country Life* and on visits to country houses for that magazine I thought that a number worth reproducing together probably existed, and so I started a notebook, which I hoped might grow into a book one day. Over a period of five years I saw more pictures than I expected, and once I began to organize the material and chase up clues provided by friends, it became clear that the number in existence was quite considerable; and obviously there must be a great many more good illustrations unknown to me.

Many of the pictures have little claim to be considered as serious art, but that is not why they have been chosen. Of course there are exceptions: occasionally Turner painted marvellous evocations of rooms, as at Petworth. But he was not primarily concerned with the details that intrigued topographical artists or amateurs, and it is their work that provides the most vivid illustrations for those interested in domestic life or decoration in the first decades of the 19th century. As we shall see, the period is a comparatively narrow one, and these illustrations amount to a minor genre that owes something to the Georgian conversation piece, rather more to early 19th century narrative painting, and its virtual end to photography. However, simply because so many of the pictures are the earnest and rather artless results of the amateur's patience they have a particular kind of appeal, bringing to life rooms that have been destroyed, altered or often left virtually unused for two generations. They are complementary to descriptions in letters, diaries, topographical publications and novels, and so form part of the patchwork of leisured life in England over a hundred years ago.

Originally I had planned that the book would cover a broader period, carrying the story on until the present day, but in the end size forced me to concentrate on a shorter one in order to get as full a representation of those decades as possible and so, hopefully, make it more useful to restorers and designers. Ideally there should have been comparative illustrations as well, but again, because it was intended to be primarily a picture book with explanatory notes and not an introduction to the history of furniture and decoration, they had to be omitted. I hope the book fills out aspects of *English Decoration in the 18th Century* and that it will be a bridge to an expanded edition taking the story down to the middle of the 19th century.

LIST OF ILLUSTRATIONS

INTRODUCTION

Were the English stoics until servants vanished and oil-fired central heating was invented? This question would make a nice interdisciplinary study, but while waiting for it and while our boilers are turned down, or off, to save on running costs, childhood memories are being revived in many houses. Once more we can feel for Lady Belgrave dreading going to stay with her parents-in-law in the 1820s at Eaton Hall in Cheshire, which despite all the luxury she found as 'cold and comfortless as usual'. Reading her letters and diaries quoted by Gervas Huxley in *Lady Elizabeth and the Grosvenors*, such a phrase leaps out from the page and makes one wonder about the realities of life in houses 150 years ago.

In the 1950s and 60s comfort and convenience came to be thought of as such basic attributes of a house large or small that they were taken for granted and their absence regarded as regrettable, even eccentric. Questions were, and are, seldom asked about their origin and development, or, to be more precise, about changing attitudes to them in the past, when the emphasis was on dignity and magnificence rather than ease and informality. Certainly the discomfort of display has been neglected, but the history of domestic architecture has been written in such a way that only recently have there been moves to consider it in terms other than that of stylistic development. This broadening of approach is still in its early stages, involving as it does a reconsideration of planning, more research into the design and use of furniture, understanding social customs and practices as well as piecing together a more precise picture of the costs of living, not forgetting all the difficulties of striking a balance between what appears to have been the theory and what turns out to have been the practice. Books on etiquette of every generation, whether architectural or social, have to be treated with caution simply because, through the process of writing down advice for those who are thought to need it, the advice itself becomes too codified and formalized as well as instantly out-of-date in the circles whence it derives.

There is an almost overwhelming richness of material to draw on for 18th-century England, but even so this does not make it easy to imagine how people lived in houses and used them. Through the drawings of architects from the time of Colen Campbell onwards the ideals are known; from formal portraits the way the sitters wished to present themselves; descriptions in letters and journals help to bring to life groups in conversation pieces and silhouettes; and, of course, there are the houses themselves and the rooms that survive together with their furniture, upholstery and objects in daily use. Even so we see Georgian life as through a windowpane or reflected in a ghostly looking glass where time has crazed the silver.

Then, leaping forward to shortly after the mid-19th century, the camera's eye comes into its own, and it becomes possible to look in much greater detail at many more aspects of life through a medium that still dominates and largely conditions our way of looking around us. The window pane and the looking glass both seem to clear.

Between these two periods there is another, lasting about half a century, for which there is a surprising amount of unexplored material in the form of paintings and drawings of the English at home, many by amateurs but some by professionals. Seldom is it great art – indeed perhaps only when Turner stayed at Petworth – and frequently it

is technically incompetent; but yet just because of its simple, direct and even naive approach it has a great deal to tell about life. Some of these views of interiors have been reproduced in the past, in books and articles, and a series like Pyne's *Royal Residences* has always been justly celebrated. However, this present attempt to gather together a collection of paintings, watercolours, drawings and etchings seems to have produced its own general picture of the period – one that suggested the title for the book.

The reasons why this minor genre developed when it did and not before appear to be surprisingly involved. Leisure and a fashion for drawing lessons, illustrated books and antiquarian studies all played their part, as we shall see, but underlying them, and much more important, were fundamental changes in attitudes to concepts of home and family life, involving the status of women, and, to some extent at least, the start of a technological revolution with improvements in heating, plumbing and domestic appliances that only found complete realization in England in the 1950s and 60s.

If this sounds over-complicated, the basic message of the illustrations is one of increasing informality in the arrangement of rooms, which brings with it two half-surprises; that what is usually taken to be a specifically Victorian way of arranging and using a room appears to date from considerably earlier than the 1850s; and that the modern English country house style with its 'lived-in' look owes a great deal to the approach of people in the period 1825–45. Today formality is unfashionable, and, because the prospect of it can cause apprehension and even fear, the aim of the English country house style in recent decades has been to create a sense of informality and ease through a synthesis of furniture of different dates and styles, with deliberate contrasts between relaxing chairs and sofas and furniture that may be more formal and even grand in design and intention. The evolution of this style in the past half-century is a distinctively twentieth-century affair, the product of contemporary changes, pressures and attitudes, but once its intentions are understood the parallel with the world revealed in most of these pictures is striking. If the origins of the Modern Movement in furniture design can be traced back to the Regency period and further back to the publications of Hepplewhite and Sheraton, similarly the traditional country house style of today is also seen to owe a great deal to the same period of transition.

The preciseness, or lack of it, with which that period of transition can be defined is a problem. In late 18th-century literature there is an increasing number of remarks that suggest a greater awareness of comfort and discomfort. The first decade of the 19th century saw the introduction of new forms of furniture and in particular the Grecian couch, which was not intended to be set with its back to the wall. And by about 1810 the formal arrangement of 18th-century rooms was starting to be broken up in certain houses, but so far there is insufficient evidence for us to be definite on dates. However,

1

A DRAWING OF AN INTERIOR, *about 1630*
A puzzling drawing discovered among the Burlington Collection at Chatsworth, it appears t date from about 1630, but there is no clue as t what kind of bedroom is depicted. The classica landscape over the fireplace and the style of th carving suggests a prominent patron: on the othe hand the treatment of the walls suggests that i may have been part of a temporary building.

the change may have begun rather earlier than this, for in a letter written in 1799 by Lady Louisa Stuart to her sister Lady Portarlington, she describes Archerfield, a country house in East Lothian, as

a most excellent one, . . . and now fitted up. . . . All is new and nicely furnished in the most fashionable manner. It wants nothing but more furniture for the middle of rooms. I mean all is set out in order, no comfortable tables to write or read at; it looks like a fine London house prepared for company; quite a contrast to the delightful gallery at Dalkeith, where you can settle yourself in any corner. I wonder at this, for they are by no means formal people, and Lady Elgin was likely enough to have routed them out of any primness.

Unfortunately most of the views of interiors known at the moment seem to date from 1820 onwards rather than from 1800. On the other hand there is no reason to suppose that a picture of 1820, 1830 or 1840 is necessarily a record of a recent change or arrangement; and it is only on specific occasions that certain professional views are of new rooms. English decorators do not appear to have provided complete perspectives of the furnished rooms they were proposing, and Gillow's idiosyncratic room plans showing the furniture appear to be unique to that firm. Indeed what is striking about most of the pictures is that frequently the contents of a room can be proved to date back twenty to thirty years or more. Also, it has to be remembered that the appearance of a room depended, as it still does, not only on the personality and means of the owner but also on his or her age, so that it may have borne no resemblance to what was considered fashionable at the time the record was made. A house or a room is seldom a fixed entity, and in the late 18th and early 19th century a new room did not necessarily mean new furniture. These illustrations, in fact, depict what would be expected, that most houses consisted of a mixture of things acquired at different times and put together as happily – or unhappily – as may be. The room furnished in the style of one particular period was always the exception.

However, bearing in mind these gaps and qualifications, the apparently straightforward Regency style is marked by fundamental changes that are more difficult to pin down than might be imagined, changes connected with the passing of the initiative in matters of patronage and design from the aristocracy to the upper middle classes. In the early 19th century the landed aristocracy was as rich as ever and getting even richer, and its members were determined to keep ahead of those with newer fortunes through conspicuous expenditure, as can be seen in pictures and correspondence relating to houses like Eaton Hall and Stafford House in London. But when they ordered new furniture it was usually more elaborate and costly versions of what was intended for the upper middle class rather than the other way about, as had been the situation thirty to fifty years before, when middle-class furniture was a simplification of designs made for the aristocracy. Chippendale, like Adam, had aimed for the top of the market and won it, while not neglecting bread-and-butter jobs. Hepplewhite and Sheraton were primarily publicists aiming at a different level, and the importance of publications like Thomas Hope's *Household Furniture and Interior Decoration* and George Smith's *Collection of Designs for Household Furniture* lay in their increasingly broad appeal. Hope himself was a bridge figure, a member of a banking family eager to

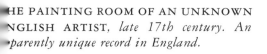

THE PAINTING ROOM OF AN UNKNOWN ENGLISH ARTIST, *late 17th century. An apparently unique record in England.*

establish a position for himself in London social and artistic life, but having special objects made to order in the aristocratic tradition with the intention of improving public taste and standards of design.

A new degree of mechanization in furniture making had much to do with the new kind of market that was aimed at, and as yet this is perhaps more clearly understood in relation to Biedermeier than to Regency furniture, because in England the tendency is still to look at the furniture of this period in terms of what was supplied to and survives in large and rare settled houses like Southill in Bedfordshire. Splendid as this often is, it is not necessarily more original in conception than much simpler and cheaper furniture that has been studied less because it has lost its provenance and so is undocumented.

It was partly in an attempt to keep ahead that the aristocracy and their advisers pursued the Louis Revival in the years after Waterloo, because, as B. D. Wyatt told Lord and Lady Stafford, it was a style that defied cheap imitation. The Louis Revival, and with it the acquisition of genuine Louis XIV and Louis XV furniture, dovetailed in with a growing taste for historical pieces of all kinds and in particular for the Old English Style that had been gaining ground during the Napoleonic Wars, when even the Prince of Wales had to control his French enthusiasm for patriotic reasons. And both, of course, ran counter to what Hope was trying to do for the improvement of public taste. Recently there has been an increasing interest in both the Louis Revival and the Old English Style, and not least the interesting aspect of the illustrations of rooms is the way they reveal how widespread these two styles both were.

If the Regency style, despite its linkage of name with that of the Prince Regent and his extravagance as a patron of furniture makers and decorators, was not really a palace or great house style, it may be because the great house was a more or less obsolete form by the end of the 18th century. The villa, whether in the Palladian tradition or in the rising Picturesque fashion, was essentially domestic and intimate. Nash and Repton's development of the Picturesque villa in the opening years of the 19th century was primarily a matter of relationship between architecture and landscape, both in the way the house looked in its setting and in the way the views from the house were contrived. Such considerations were as important as, and indeed they may have been more important than, those of internal arrangements and the relationships of rooms.

It is hard to find the right kind of documentary evidence to support this interpreta-
tion, but it is surely no accident that the appearance of the Picturesque villa and the
break-up of Georgian formality of furniture arrangement occurred at more or less the
same time – about 1800–1810. It was as if people, having become aware of the chill of
state rooms and the inconvenience of having to be attended by servants to set out the
chairs, discovered how to live more agreeably and informally in fewer and smaller
rooms. Repton expressed this best, and it is a matter of regret that he did not write
more fully on 'living-rooms' and publish more model houses like Armley Hall in
Yorkshire and Sheringham in Norfolk.

The development of villa design and changes in furniture arrangement amounted to
a near-revolution, but it is also relevant here that there had been another related
revolution a few years earlier, in costume design. The most dramatic innovation had
been the dress à la Grecque in 1793, the year of Robespierre's death, but even before
the outbreak of the French Revolution French fashion had been simplified under the
influence of English styles in the 1770s and 80s with their emphasis on cut. As the
Cunningtons have written of Beau Brummel, his 'conception of a gentleman's clothes
was, in fact, a fundamental change from a pictorial design to an architectural one; from
composition in colours to one in lines, marking a progress from a crude to a subtle
method of expressing social superiority'.

It is not the aim of this book to investigate the development of costume design any
more than it is to follow that of architectural or furniture design, but the links are too
important to overlook. The Grecian couch, for instance, suggests reclining, and
reclining in a different kind of dress from that fashionable in the mid-18th century
when skirts were full; the narrowness of both male and female costume is reflected in
the proportions of Regency chairs, with or without arms; and the habit of placing a sofa
table in front of a sofa suggests ease of sitting down in such a position, a feat difficult to
manage in earlier styles.

All this comes into sharper focus in Walter Houghton's *The Victorian Frame of Mind
1830–70*, where he quotes from the writings of J. S. Mill in 1869.

The association of men with women in daily life [wrote Mill], is much closer and more complete than it
had been ever before. Men's life is more domestic. Formerly, their pleasures and chosen occupations
were among men, and in men's company: their wives had but a fragment of their lives. At the present time,
the progress of civilisation and the turn of opinion against the rough amusements and convivial excesses
which formerly occupied most men in their hours of relaxation – together with (it must be said) the
improved tone of modern feeling as to the reciprocity of duty which binds the husband towards the wife –
have thrown the man very much upon the home and its inmates, for his personal and social pleasures.

Walter Houghton himself wrote: 'At the centre of Victorian life was the family. . . .
Since women have always been concerned with the home this special development in
the Victorian period must be attributed to a re-orientation of the masculine attitude.'
Also, as he says, life became more domestic because of the existence of larger families,
and men were required to give more time and attention to the home.

In his *Victorian Country House* Mark Girouard takes the point further and contrasts
'the [Regency] Man of Taste [who] was personally involved with his house as an
expression of his sensibility', and 'the Victorian gentleman' to whom 'his house was (or
ought to be) a temple not of taste but of the domestic virtues. . . .'

A gentleman's house should be substantial, serious and preferably in a style associated with the traditions
of English country life. It should be dignified, as was suitable for the rank of its owner, but not
ostentatious; designed for family life and the entertainment of friends rather than for show. It should
provide decent quarters for servants. It should protect the womanliness of women and encourage the
manliness of man. It should be comfortable but not luxurious.

It is this kind of spirit that is implicit in most of the illustrations in this book, whether
they are of rooms in houses old or new. And of course they are often not just records
of rooms but of family life, of talking, sewing, reading, painting and so on, often at the
same time and in a way that is virtually never seen today. Perhaps the parts of the
houses where female influence was dominant tend to be the most frequently recorded
just because most of the amateur artists were women, but there are enough views of
billiard rooms to suggest the tendency of rooms in 19th-century houses to take on
specialized uses, with fairly clearly defined parts of a house where family and guests
mingled, where the family retreated, where the men did not expect to be disturbed,
and, of course, the equally elaborate arrangements for the servants that are not
recorded here but can be gathered from the complex plans of Victorian houses.
Inevitably a collection of views of the kind gathered together here must be akin to that
of a scrapbook, and in an attempt to give a degree of cohesion this introduction will
end with a series of contemporary quotations that cannot be directly illustrated but
complement the illustrations that follow.

However, before coming to the quotations it is necessary to consider the genre as a
whole and try to work out why such views are such a rarity before 1800, and why a
hundred years separates the two drawings of Samuel Pepys's book room (Plates 101

and 102) which appear to be the earliest accurate record of an identified English interior, and the series of views of Strawberry Hill done by Edward Edwards in 1781 and by Carter seven years later (Plates 127–132). Surely the absence of more drawings is surprising considering the English passion for building throughout the 18th century with its concentration on the private house? Why did the English not record their rooms, particularly in view of their interest in pictures of the outsides of their houses and those showing the relationship of houses to their setting?

One obvious approach to this is through attitudes to painting and to architecture and decoration from the mid-16th century onwards. For at least a hundred years after the Reformation, English painting was not only dominated by portraiture but was virtually confined to it. Only very gradually did topographical and sporting painting develop in the second half of the 17th century; and pure landscape only became a recognizable genre in the early 18th century. The backgrounds of even the most spectacular full-length Elizabethan and Jacobean portraits seldom do more than suggest the richness of their sitters through the inclusion of an oriental carpet, the trimming on a chair, embroidery on a cushion, fringing on a tablecloth or alternating panels of damask and cut velvet. It is rare to find a figure set in even a formalized room, and in the best known example, Eworth's portrait of the Earls of Darnley and Lennox in the Royal Collection, painted in 1563, the design of the room is taken from a print by Vriedeman de Vries published about three years earlier. There is nothing in England comparable with those 17th-century pictures of galleries and cabinets associated with the Archduke Leopold, the backgrounds to Mytens's celebrated portraits of the Earl and Countess of Arundel being suggestions rather than accurate records of galleries at Arundel House. And portraiture tended to be even less specific in its background details throughout the century dominated by Van Dyck, Lely and Kneller.

If there was no tradition of subject painting, of depicting incidents or stories in convincing settings as in Holland, architectural draughtsmanship was equally restricted until the late 17th century, and indeed most of the time it was surprisingly crude. The one great exception to this, of course, was Inigo Jones, whose drawings are among the most beautiful ever done in England, but even he with all his experience of the theatre never seems to have made complete designs for rooms or perspectives of interiors.

It seems that it was Daniel Marot, the Franco–Dutch designer who came to England with William and Mary, who produced the first decorative schemes with not only walls and ceilings, but hangings, beds, seat furniture and details of upholstery. However, despite the considerable influence of his style in England, his method of presenting his interiors does not seem to have been imitated at all. Instead the bird's-eye views of *Britannia Illustrata* were developed into the more finely engraved elevations and sections of *Vitruvius Britannicus*, and it was the plates in the latter that became the accepted way of presenting architectural interiors for some seventy years. Designs for ceilings, chimneypieces and door cases occur in all the principal books, with Vardy's *Designs of Mr Inigo Jones and of Mr William Kent* (1744) being the first major English architectural book to include specific furniture designs. The first influential English book of furniture designs was Chippendale's *Director* (1754), but despite its full title

plasterwork in the time of the Fifth Lord Byron, the great-uncle of the poet. When the latter came of age in 1808, he found the old house neglected and bare, but whether the Great Room was as completely empty as Grimm depicts it is unknown. The second drawing, attributed to Henry Shaw, shows the same room after Byron had sold the Abbey to Colonel Wildman, who employed John Shaw to restore the house for him. There is no connection between the Shaws, and the reason for the second drawing is not known.

The Gentleman and Cabinet-Maker's Director it was intended for cabinet-makers rather than upholsterers, so that a contemporary would have been hard put to do a complete room following his book. For example, he shows pelmet cornices without giving clues as to how to cut the curtains or fix them.

Robert Adam's *Works in Architecture* followed the established formula, but he included a greater range of details, arranging them in a formal pattern deriving from the engravings of Piranesi. However, he did include a few rooms represented in a three-dimensional way, among them the Drawing Room at Derby House, Grosvenor Square, and the Gallery at Syon House; but no furniture was shown, and the rooms were treated as architectural perspectives in the form continued by Thomas Malton (Plate 64).

This absence of furniture seems surprising in view of the fashion for the conversation piece, with its depiction of people in what are usually thought to be accurate settings. A great many 18th-century conversation pieces have been reproduced, but with remarkably few exceptions the rooms as opposed to the details are not convincing, and it is probably not safe to place too much reliance on them. Certain details of upholstery and furnishing can be regarded as satisfactory documents, but Arthur Devis, for instance, who is often regarded as a valuable recorder because of his evident simplicity, seems highly suspect: like an Edwardian photographer he may well have had a selection of backgrounds to offer his sitters. Exactly the same 'room', for instance, appears in both *The Fleetwood Family* and *The Cholmondeley Family*. In Sir Roger Newdigate's portrait the library at Arbury is accurately depicted, but the lack of relationship between the sitter and the setting suggests that the artist may have married up the two, possibly taking the setting from a specially prepared architectural perspective. At first sight Zoffany appears more truthful, and the temptation is to take his portraits of *Queen Charlotte, Sir Lawrence Dundas* and *The Willoughby de Broke Family* at their face value, particularly as some of the objects can still be identified, but his Towneley picture is a caprice and it appears that there are serious problems about the Dundas picture as well. It is because of this doubt surrounding most 18th-century conversation pictures that virtually all are omitted from this book.

The conversation piece was a much more popular form of portraiture in England than in France, but against that there was no real English equivalent of the French pictures and prints by Lavreince and J. B. Mallet usually showing moments of inconvenient discovery, with bed curtains flying and little tables toppled on their sides. Quite apart from their mildly titillating themes, the details of informality are of great interest and are much more convincing than anything to be seen in English painting at the same period; they relate to impressions to be gained from letters, and to some extent they anticipate the illustrations chosen for this book rather better than conversation pieces.

The conversation piece and the risqué French print may seem a digression from the prim Robert Adam and his presentation of interiors, but what Adam and his contemporaries did establish was the practice of making coloured designs, particularly for interiors. However, while Adam had a few coloured copies of his *Works* prepared, the coloured architectural plate remained a near-impossibility until the development of the coloured aquatint and its use for book illustration in the 1790s. Much of the credit for this form of publishing belongs to Rudolph Ackermann, and it was the success of books like his *Microcosm of London*, published in 1808–11, that inspired Pyne to embark on his *Royal Residences*. We are so familiar with Pyne's plates that it is hard to realize what a novel kind of view they were when first published. Even so they cannot be considered in isolation, because they interlocked not only with the fashion for antiquarian studies and publications but with the acquisition of the habit of travelling for pleasure by a broader range of people, many of whom were also fairly new to regular book buying.

It was all part of that growing prosperity of the age to be seen not only in the increasingly large fortunes of the few but in the increase in the numbers of those who were well-to-do, people with leisure and able to spend more on their houses. Ackermann, like Wedgwood a generation earlier, seems to have understood the new situation and saw the opening for a magazine like the *Repository of Arts*, which he started in 1809. Thus a new kind of market coincided with economies in furniture making, and what was arguably a more standardized taste was moulded by new publications.

The spread in the fashion for lessons in drawing and painting was one result of this prosperity and leisure. What had begun earlier as a practical skill to help a landowner in the improvement of his house and estate had become a popular hobby whereby both ladies and gentlemen could express their sensibility to landscape and nature. Writers on the Picturesque opened their eyes, and their enthusiasm was encouraged by tours of the Lake District and the Wye and by illustrations in books. Also many of the leading watercolourists in the second half of the 18th century and at the beginning of the 19th century gave drawing lessons: Alexander Cozens, for instance, taught the young William Beckford, Thomas Girtin taught Edward Lascelles at Harewood and J. S. Cotman the Cholmeleys of Brandsby. It is a tribute to the excellence of the instruction that a surprising number of their leisured pupils became proficient, if not exactly inspired, artists, and in certain families a tradition was established that lasted two and even three generations.

Eighteenth-century amateurs were primarily moved by nature and by a literary approach to painting that was in the classical tradition; and it was only in the wake of professional artists who began to paint scenes of everyday life, partly inspired by contemporary interest in the 17th-century Dutch School, that amateurs in the early 19th century seem to have lowered their sights to record the houses and gardens where they spent their lives. Mountains and rivers may have remained the ideal subjects, but on many a rainy day amateur artists brought out their watercolours in the drawing room and the conservatory.

A lowering of sights and a new interest in the pictorial possibilities of daily life must be part of the explanation of why there seem to be suddenly so many illustrations of interiors after 1820, but it is not the whole explanation. As well as handsome topographical books with aquatint illustrations, there were a surprising number of guidebooks to country houses in the 18th century, and starting with Strawberry Hill in 1784, illustrated with plates of the interior after Edwards's drawings, there developed a fashion for more elaborate monographs illustrated with aquatints, etchings, engravings and later lithographs. There are about fifteen well-known ones, starting with Hope's *Household Furniture and Interior Decoration* (1807); this was followed by T. L. Parker's *Browsholme* (1815), the Bucklers' *Eaton Hall* of 1826; John Britton's *Cassiobury* of 1837; his *Toddington* of 1840; the Rev. Arundell's *History of Cotehele* of about 1840; and Richard Ford's memorial volume, *Walmer Castle and Apsley House*, in 1853. In addition there were the three parts of P. F. Robinson's abortive *Vitruvius Britannicus, Woburn* coming out in 1827, *Hardwick* in 1833 and *Hatfield* in 1835.

Britton, in his introductions to *Cassiobury* and *Toddington*, explains the background of such works, referring to the appearance of monographs with and without plates and saying of Robinson's *Vitruvius Britannicus*: 'Its size and price are obstacles to popularity: for the present age is an age of cheap literature and cheap embellishment.' In his earlier introduction to his *Sir John Soane's House* in 1827 he wrote: 'Till lately, interior architecture, which is certainly of the very first importance in a country where the climate compels us to seek our social engagements and relaxations within our dwellings, has not been sufficiently attended to by the higher class of architects, nor has it formed the subject of any graphic work.'

Improving public taste, providing a historical record and flattering owners all played their part in the genesis of these books, but certainly vanity was the least important of the three, probably only counting in the Bucklers' *Eaton Hall*. Improving public taste influenced Hope, Soane and Britton. Serious historical research tinged with romanticism inspired Parker's *Browsholme* and Joseph Skelton's catalogue of S. R. Meyrick's collection at Goodrich Court. The later books also coincided with the first books on

VII

CHARLES TOWNELEY IN HIS LIBRARY AT PARK STREET, WESTMINSTER, *by Zoffany, 1782. Until recently it was generally thought that Zoffany's conversation pieces were likely to be the most accurate pictures of contemporary rooms, but it is now realised that while he depicted objects accurately his compositions were as carefully arranged as in architectural* capriccios.

VIII

SIR ROWLAND AND LADY WYNN IN THE LIBRARY AT NOSTELL PRIORY, YORKSHIRE. The picture was painted by an unrecorded artist apparently immediately after the completion of the room in August, 1767. Sir Rowland had succeeded in 1765 and received Robert Adam's design the following year. Work went ahead, and Chippendale's bill for the library table is dated 1767. The picture shows Adam's original colour scheme described in his instructions, but the artist has altered the scale of the room depicting two pedimented units, where in fact there is only a single one. The placing of the furniture is also purely pictorial.

old English furniture, a tradition established by Henry Shaw, whose *Specimens of Ancient Furniture* appeared in 1836.

But the genre might not have developed quite in the way it did if certain patrons and professional artists had not had such close connections. Indeed the group of illustrations here brings out the intimacy of society at the time. Among the patrons T. L. Parker of Browsholme and Sir John Leicester were friends and both knew Sir Richard Colt Hoare of Stourhead. Buckler and Britton were evidently on good terms with Mr Parker and Lord Essex; Meyrick wrote the notes for Shaw's *Ancient Furniture*; earlier Shaw had been employed as a draughtsman by Britton, advised Lord Braybrooke at Audley End and did plates for Robinson. Thus there was a fairly solid core of people who were interested in more or less the same thing at the same time, several being members of the Society of Antiquaries, and this no doubt inspired others not only to copy their illustrations but to think more deeply about their houses and what they stood for. And conceivably this in its way contributed to what has come to be identified as the specifically Victorian attitude to the house and home.

This explanation of how and why the genre developed when it did may or may not be convincing, but even if it is it does not explain how houses worked in the 19th century. However, with the aid of fairly long descriptions at least a general picture can be attempted, which may throw light on details in some of the illustrations that follow and help to bring them to life. The impressions of foreigners are particularly valuable, some of the most vivid being those of the Polish adventurer Prince Puckler-Muskau, who came to England in search of a rich wife to stave off a disastrous collapse in his fortunes. Among the great houses he stayed in was Cobham Hall in Kent, then the seat of the Earl of Darnley, and he wrote a long account of the '*vie de château*' to his old mistress.

It forms, without any question [he wrote on 3 February 1827] the most agreeable side of English life; for there is great freedom, and a banishment of most of the wearisome ceremonies which, with us, tire both host and guest. . . .

Strangers have generally only one room allotted to them, usually a spacious apartment on the first floor. Englishmen seldom go into this room except to sleep, and to dress twice a day, which even without company and in the most strictly domestic circles, is always 'de rigueur'; for all meals are commonly taken in company, and any one who wants to write does it in the library. There, also, those who wish to converse give each other 'rendezvous', to avoid either the whole society, or particular parties, in the formation of which people are quite at liberty. Here you may have an opportunity of gossiping for hours with the young ladies, who are always very literarily inclined. . . .

Ten or eleven is the hour for breakfast, at which you may appear in 'négligé'. It is always of the same kind I described to you in the inn, only of course more elegant and complete. The ladies do the honours of the table very agreeably. If you come down later, when the breakfast is removed, a servant brings you what you want . . . and about half an hour before dinner the company meet again in the drawing-room in elegant toilette. . . .

At the second breakfast, the 'luncheon', which is served a few hours after the first, and is generally eaten only by the women (who like to make 'la petite bouche' at dinner), there are no napkins, and altogether less neatness and elegance than at the other meals. [He describes dinner elsewhere.] When you enter, you find the whole of the first course on the table as in France.

After the soup is removed, and the covers are taken off, every man helps the dish before him, and offers some of it to his neighbour; if he wishes for anything else, he must ask across the table, or send a servant for it. . . .

It is not usual to take wine without drinking to another person. When you raise your glass, you look fixedly at the one with whom you are drinking, bow your head, and then drink with the greatest gravity.

. . . If the company is small, and a man has drunk with everybody, but happens to wish for more wine, he must wait for the dessert, if he does not find in himself courage to brave custom.

At the conclusion of the second course comes a sort of intermediate dessert of cheese, butter, salad, raw celery, and the like; after which ale, sometimes 30 or 40 years old, and so strong that when thrown upon the fire it blazes like spirit, is handed about. The tablecloth is then removed: under it, at the best tables, is a finer, upon which the dessert is set. At inferior ones, it is placed on the bare polished table. . . . After the dessert is set on, all the servants leave the room: if more is wanted the bell is rung, and the butler alone brings it in. The ladies sit a quarter of an hour longer, during which time sweet wines are sometimes served, and then rise from the table. . . . Every man is, however, at liberty to follow the ladies as soon as he likes. . . .

[And to return to the *'vie de château'* at Cobham.] A light supper of cold meats and fruits is brought, at which everyone helps himself, and shortly after midnight all retire. A number of small candlesticks stand ready on a side-table; every man takes his own, and lights himself up to bed; for the greater part of the servants, who have to rise up early, are, as is fair and reasonable, gone to bed. The eternal sitting of servants in an ante-room is not the custom here; and except at appointed times, when their services are expected, they are little seen, and one waits on oneself.

At night I found a most excellent chintz bed with a canopy. It was so enormously large that I lay like an icicle in it, – for the distant fire was too remote to give any sensible warmth.

The Prince's account is unusually long and vivid, and the way of life does not seem to have been in any way untypical of the time and it can be confirmed from the accounts of other writers.

Two accounts of dinner are worth quoting here, one by Mrs Bancroft and one by another American, Anna Maria Fay, who went to Oakly Park near Ludlow in 1852. Mrs Bancroft's hostess was old Lady Charleville – she was eighty-four – and 'at table she helped to the fish and insisted on carving the turkey herself'.

The four *entrée* dishes are always placed on the table when we sit down, according to our old fashion, and not one by one. They have [them] warmed with hot water, so that they keep hot while the soup and fish are eaten. Turkey, even *boiled* turkey, is brought *after* the *entrées*, mutton (a saddle always) or venison, with a pheasant or partridges. With the roast is always put on the *sweets*, as they are called, as the true dessert seems restricted to the last course of fruits. During the dinner there are always long strips of damask all round the table which are removed before the dessert is put on, and there is no brushing of crumbs.

Anna Marie Fay dined at Oakly Park on New Year's Day 1852, and, having arrived with a beating heart at the door, as she describes in *Victorian Days in England*, continued:

Two footmen in red plush breeches and blue coats and silver buttons, and the groom of the chambers in black, received us in the vestibule, where we took off our cloaks. The dignitary in black preceded us through the hall and throwing open the door announced us as Mr and Mrs Fay, and the Misses Fays and Mr Fay. We found ourselves in a large and beautiful library, an elegant circle of ladies and gentlemen rose to meet us. Lady Harriet [Clive] received us with great dignity, and though no one was introduced every one spoke to us. It was not until the end of the evening that we knew who comprised the party. . . .

And having gone into dinner she described the table, in the centre of which

was a gilt plateau on which stood two immense candelabras with ornaments of china figures. At each end of the table were two candelabras on stands similar though smaller than the plateau. The effect produced by these four candelabras filled with wax candles, and the beaming light thrown upon everyone was very fine. The pantry butler in white vest and cravat and black coat, and the groom of the chambers, and a half dozen or more footmen in red plush and blue coats gave great elegance to the whole effect. I cannot tell you how many kinds of soup there were. Suffice it, that mine was delicious. Then followed several varieties of fish. The turbot was placed before Mr Clive. After that came little entrées, delicious patés, and mutton chops well served. On the side table were every variety of meat – turkeys, chicken, anything you could wish. These courses over, the game followed. I should have told you that the vegetables were cucumbers and asparagus. The service was entirely of silver. The dessert service was of pretty china, but nothing remarkable. The ices and jellies and other most beautifully arranged and delicious dishes were placed on the table. The dessert was composed of every variety of fruit, oranges, pears, grapes, etc. . . . Sitting a little while after dessert, Lady Harriet gave the signal to rise and we left the room. . . . We entered the large and elegant drawing room. Coffee was brought in, and some of the ladies sat down to their beautiful worsted work, while others disposed themselves around the room. . . .

Descriptions like these give a good picture of the English at home in the first half of the 19th century, but possibly the fullest account of an ideal villa of the time is that contributed anonymously to Loudon's *Encyclopedia* of 1833. Unfortunately it is too long to quote in full, but it makes a very interesting comparison with that given by Robert Kerr in his much better known book *Complete Gentleman's House* of 1864. Both accounts are in a sense etiquette books because they are very concerned with the owner creating the right kind of impression, and so both have to be taken with caution. On the other hand it is remarkable how many points made by Loudon's contributor are to be found in the illustrations here or in surviving houses. The author takes the interior of the house room by room, starting with the Entrance Hall:

If the apartments are small and devoid of ornament, I would then substitute for the hall a smaller kind of entrance, with a vaulted roof, and, moreover rather gloomy, to increase the general effect of the rooms which open into it.

For a hall in the old English style – he devoted a great deal of space to the style – he suggested

Window curtains of cloth of the simplest form. . . . The walls, painted to imitate stone, might be hung with a few of the oldest family portraits, the founder in the panel over the fireplace; and a few other pictures,

X and X

THE LETTER OF INTRODUCTION, *by David Wilkie. Wilkie (1785–1841) combined an admiration for Dutch and Flemish subject and narrative painting and classical methods of preparation with a particular interest in furniture that is best illustrated in* The Letter of Introduction *painted in 1813. Inspired by his own introduction to Caleb Whiteford when he first came to London, he shows the seated figure in a mid-eighteenth century chair covered with contemporary needlework that came from a set now at Balcarres, Fife. The same chair appears in the portrait Andrew Geddes painted of him in 1816. However, what is even more interesting is to compare the finished* Letter of Introduction *with the sketch for it. The former shows a similar disposition of bookcase, chair and desk, but in the sketch the desk is a Louis XVI cylinder top and the chair Empire, but for the finished picture Wilkie creates an old fashioned air by using his own chair and a less sophisticated English drop front desk and including beyond it an earlier Chinese lacquer cabinet.*

such as hunting pieces, Dutch fairs and other amusing subjects. To assist in furnishing the walls, armour and curious specimens of defensive arms and ancient sporting weapons, together with the horns of stags and other animals taken in the chase, might be hung around.... The family arms, and the arms of those connected with the family, should be among the ornaments of the hall.... To make the hall comfortable, it should be warmed with hot air, to which, on state occasions, I would add a fire of large logs with wood, burnt upon handsome dogs in the open chimney....

This last sentence strikes an unfamiliar note, introducing both the new technology and the passing of older ways, the fire becoming a symbol of hospitality rather than a necessity. The actual treatment of the room might well be a description of what George Lucy did at Charlecote in the 1830s or a less serious version of what T. L. Parker had done at Browsholme about twenty-five years before. By the 1830s the neo-classical style was beginning to seem an all-too-chilly alternative, and it was typical of the suggestions for the treatment of the hall in a Greek-style house that in winter 'a few strips of India matting between the doors of the rooms would give it an appearance of comfort'.

The craze for ebony and ebonized furniture of the kind admired by Horace Walpole and later by Beckford, and so eagerly bought up at the Fonthill sale by George Lucy, was already fairly widespread, for in the Gallery, a broad corridor leading off the hall, the author proposed 'a few ebony chairs and settees, with a table or two, against the side opposite the windows, which should have curtains, without draperies, of crimson cloth'.

The Gallery was envisaged as leading into the Saloon, which was evidently no longer as important as it had been in Palladian days, for he defined it as 'generally a sort of vestibule to the living-rooms'. He would not have the ceiling white, as would be presumed today, but 'a warm fawn colour might be the ground of the whole painting', which he envisaged as being picked out to reflect the pattern of the ribs. The carpet, also surprisingly, he recommended to be 'of thin material ... showing about a yard all round it of the polished oak boards', itself an interesting reference to the reaction against dry scrubbing fashionable in the 18th century.

It should, of course, be a bordered carpet; the colour of the ground a shade of fawn; the pattern chiefly shades of crimson. The curtains I would have of crimson watered silk, without draperies, supported by large rods of gilt brass, with handsome knobs. The chairs and seats should be without cushions, and of rather a plain description, so as not to interfere with the splendid effect of the drawing-room.... In arranging the contents of the room, a crowded effect of furniture is to be especially avoided, as being at variance with an air of dignity and elegance which is proper to the saloon.

This last is surely a remarkable warning to find in 1833 and, save for the evidence of the illustration here, might well be thought to date from the late 1840s or more likely the 1850s.

'Though two drawing-rooms are necessary in a London house,' he wrote, 'one will be found sufficient in an ordinary country residence, containing a saloon and library, as the latter would be used as the family sitting-room on common occasions,' a practice suggested by Repton and widely adopted to judge from the illustrations here. After describing the contrasting views from the windows over the park and the parterre, an arrangment to be paralleled in the Library at Scotney Castle designed by Salvin five years later, he goes on to suggest 'a splendid white marble chimneypiece, copied from one of the most magnificent designs common in old English houses', unpainted woodwork, preferably polished oak (which would have probably turned out a sticky chocolate or sharp ginger displeasing to 20th-century eyes) and 'some contrast between the colour of the walls and curtains'; but he pointed out that 'where silk or velvet is used for the furniture of a room, a papered wall has generally a poor effect.' He would hang 'some of the finest pictures that were not of a large size', itself a suggestion that would appear to be different from that likely in the 18th century when the object would have been to create a strong pattern through the close hanging of a number of pictures, including some large ones for preference. He envisaged fringed curtains with simple draperies in large folds, hung from massive gilded pelmet cornices, with under-curtains of figured muslin edged with fringe to match the main curtains and other upholstery. As against the thin carpet in the saloon, here should be an Axminster carpet and rug, and the seat furniture was to be of great variety, 'large reposing chairs, others with and without arms, some of the lighter kind with gilded cane seats, and others which unite into a kind of sofa against the wall'; in addition there would be two sofas flanking the fireplace. 'A large round table is usually placed in the middle of the drawing room, in which are generally books, prints and other things to amuse the company. . . . The chief thing to be avoided in the disposition of the article, is a vulgar crowded effect; everything should seem to contribute to comfort or amusement and there should be nothing superfluous.' Finally he said, 'I would light the room entirely with wax, to the exclusion of oil, which always produces both smoke and an unpleasant smell.

In the Library he suggested substantial furniture, hangings of a warm but dark colour, and a large Turkey or Axminster carpet with 'an abundance of various sorts of seats and tables, made of some dark wood, the more carved the better. . . . The patterns of the chairs should be old fashioned; and some real old high-backed chairs might be introduced with very good effect . . .' and

as nothing gives a more dismal effect than an appearance of idleness, everything should be so arranged, both here and in the drawing-room, as if the persons using the rooms had been employed in some way or other. This effect would be produced by the daily papers, and some periodical works, and open letters received in the morning, on the principal tables; and, on other tables some of the blotting books might be open: the inkstands not thoroughly in order, with some unfinished writing and open books or portfolios, would give at least the appearance of industry. . . .

If all this sounds rather contrived, it is graphic evidence of the desire for what we often call the 'lived-in look', and it also bears out the impression of activity conveyed by many of the amateur drawings of family life in the Library.

The substantial character of the Library was transformed into magnificence in the Dining Room with its old oak wainscot re-used, its curtains of crimson velvet trimmed with gold lace and fringe and its carved and gilt pelmet cornices. Either side of the door would be carved mahogany sideboards, and in addition there would be two side tables; 'one might be a hot table, on which to put the vegetables, etc., during dinner; the other for cold meat, and the things usually kept upon this side table.' He also recommended a horseshoe wine table that could also be used for fireside dining in very cold weather; and also a crimson leather easy chair each side of the fireplace. Several of the drawings show such chairs, but probably few survive *in situ* today, two prominent ones to go in recent years being the early 19th-century chairs from the dining room at Heveningham.

Solidity was thought an integral part of the Old English style, but none of the rooms proposed in Loudon's book was an extreme example of this taste, and so it is interesting to be able to compare Washington Irving's description of his bedroom at Newstead, published in 1835, with that in the *Encyclopedia*. By then Newstead had been sold by Lord Byron to Colonel Wildman, and the latter had done a great deal to play up its historic character, as can be seen from this account.

The lower part of the walls were panelled with ancient oak, the upper part hung with Gobelin tapestry, representing Oriental hunting scenes, wherein the figures were the size of life, and of great vivacity of attitude and colour. The furniture was antique, dignified, and cumberous. High-backed chairs curiously carved, and wrought in needlework; a massive clothes-press, of dark oak, well polished, and inlaid with landscapes of variously tinted woods; a bed of state, ample and lofty, so as to be ascended by a movable flight of steps, the huge posts supporting a high tester with a towering tuft of crimson plumes at each corner, and rich curtains of crimson damask hanging in broad and heavy folds. . . .

It was evidently a Romantic assembly of objects of different dates and places of origin,

XI

THE ARRIVAL OF COUNTRY RELATIONS,
by A. Carse. Carse was a minor Scottish painter
influenced by Wilkie and he makes this unusually accurate rendering of a middle-class interior
into a narrative picture.

a kind of approach that is illustrated on several occasions in this book, but that all too
soon was to come in for criticism from Henry Shaw in his *Specimens of Ancient
Furniture*. There he claimed to have produced a collection of period examples, adding
'In an historical composition correctness in the auxiliaries is scarcely less important
than in the more prominent parts, for the introduction of a wardrobe or a chair of the
time of Queen Anne in the representation of an apartment of the reign of Henry VI is
as glaring an error as to depict soldiers in a painting of the Battle of Crecy in the
uniform and with the weapons of the dragoon guards of the present day.'

If Shaw was on the way to the 'period-room' complex, the Newstead bedroom was
an ideal rather than one readily created in a contemporary house, and the one
envisaged in the *Encyclopedia* might have turned out to be a rather charmless apartment. 'A bedchamber should be an airy, cheerful-looking apartment, rather elegantly
furnished, but in a plainer style than the living rooms. The walls look best when
papered; the doors and woodwork painted to suit the paper. . . . I should prefer a floor
that could be washed; that is, not a polished oak floor, and would not have the whole
covered with carpet.'

Rather surprisingly he goes on to describe a bathroom as

a cheap and useful luxury, which would be considered by many persons as indispensable requisites in a
perfect villa. A room of moderate size would contain the warm and shower baths; the cold bath would be
in the park, in an ornamental building on the side of the stream. I would place the bathroom in such a
situation that it could be supplied with hot water from the offices, by means of a pipe connected with the
boiler, say in kitchen or scullery. There should also be a supply of cold water by another pipe, and a drain
to carry away the waste-water.

There is no completely logical and satisfactory way of establishing an order for the
illustrations that follow, but they have been grouped as follows: plates 1–100 are of
interiors in country houses, the first 42 being of interiors in greater houses; plates
101–126 are of interiors in London houses; plates 127–159 are of interiors in the
houses of collectors and connoisseurs; plates 160–175 are a miscellany with some
more modest interiors.

Hardwick Hall
Derbyshire

From the mid-18th century onwards, as the taste for the Picturesque, the Romantic and Olden Days gathered force, Bess of Hardwick's great house aroused increasing curiosity and wonder among travellers and visitors, and beside the descriptions of Horace Walpole in 1760, Lord Torrington in 1789 and Mrs Radcliffe in 1794 can be set the drawings of furniture and details of wood-work by S. H. Grimm in 1785. Part of the attraction was undoubtedly its presumed but totally fictional association with Mary Queen of Scots, traceable as far back as Bishop Kennet's *Memoirs of the Family of Cavendish* published in 1708. It was this that moved Mrs Radcliffe in particular to write a long and emotional impression of the wronged Queen at Hardwick. During the time of the Sixth Duke of Devonshire, who succeeded in 1811, W. H. Hunt, Henry Shaw, David Cox and Lake Price did views of the interior, and these complement the Duke's own description of the house in his *Handbook* privately printed in 1845. That book reveals in a singularly sym-pathetic way his curious mixture of gaiety and melancholy that found some relief in the almost constant alterations that he made to his numerous houses and their contents. Today there is a certain desire to see the clock at Hardwick put back to the end of the 16th and the beginning of the 17th century, but the extraordinary quality of the house, which has appealed to visitors for over 200 years, also depends on what it has received from other Cavendish houses, most notably in the Sixth Duke's time. These plates underline

that feeling for history and historic houses that was so characteristic of his generation, an approach, as Mark Girouard has said, that 'was visual and romantic rather than scholarly and historical'. It inspired not only many of the schemes illustrated in this book, but also led artists, both amateur and professional, to record them.

The plate of the High Great Chamber in P. F. Robinson's *Vitruvius Britannicus* (1835) was executed by Henry Shaw, the first man to illustrate a serious account of ancient English furniture, and consequently the detail of the furniture is very clear, particularly when compared with Lake Price's romantic ap-proach in 1858. Shaw's view is particularly valuable, because he shows at the north end of the room the embroidered canopy of estate and backcloth bearing the arms of the Second Earl of Devonshire and his wife, who married in 1608. The Sixth Duke had the canopy restored in 1844, but unfortunately after a period at Chatsworth it was later adapted for a State Bed and replaced with a new one. Beneath the canopy, flanking what could be one of the 'farthingale' chairs with arms in its original state, are a pair of carved walnut chairs of about 1700 that still retain their original upholstery of red velvet orna-mented with panels of silver embroidery; and in front stands the Elizabethan 'Eglantine' table, so called because of an inscription in the marquetry that alludes to one of the elements in the Hardwick arms. The set of long stools are 17th-century, while the two tables that flank the bay look 'Old English'.

1

THE HIGH GREAT CHAMBER AT HARDWICK HALL, DERBYSHIRE. *An engraving from* Vitruvius Britannicus *(1835) based on a drawing by Henry Shaw.*

2
THE HIGH GREAT CHAMBER. *A watercolour*
by Lake Price, 1858.

3
THE WITHDRAWING ROOM. *A watercolour*
by W. H. Hunt, 1828.

but were thought to be authentic and appear as such in Shaw's *Specimens of Ancient Furniture.* When the Duke dismantled the old Scots Rooms at Chatsworth in 1827, he decided to send over to Hardwick 'what was called' Mary Queen of Scots' State Bed and have it set up in the deep bay. He was right in his doubts because it must have been made about 1700. Only fragments of it survive.

The Duke tried to dine in the High Great Chamber and to sit in the evening in the Long Gallery, but he was driven out by the cold; eventually he made the adjoining room, originally the Withdrawing Room and then rising to the same height as the High Great Chamber, into a library. When he inherited,

it was 'nothing but a dull and dreary bedroom', and in recent years it has been the State Bedroom. W. H. Hunt's watercolour done in 1828 shows it before the Duke set up bookcases but after he had put up the alabaster relief of *Orpheus and the Muses*, originally part of Elizabethan Chatsworth. Between the windows appears one of the pieces of furniture original to the room, the Sea-Dog table, and in the centre two facing rows of mid-18th-century chairs sent down from Devonshire House in London, a type of arrangement also recorded by Pyne at Carlton House. The habit of hanging portraits in front of tapestry is now only to be found at Hardwick, but it must have been a fairly usual practice when tapestry was treated like wall-

4

THE LONG GALLERY. *A watercolour by W. H. Hunt, 1828.*

paper, and is also recorded by Pyne. On the floor can be seen some of the rush matting noted by Lord Torrington in 1789 that still remains a special feature of the house.

Hunt also painted one of the small bedrooms to the north of the Great Apartment. Called the Little Chamber in 1601, it had become associated with Mary Queen of Scots before the 1780s, when her arms over the door were sketched and described. The bed is of black velvet with Elizabethan embroidery and as it exists today is a good 19th-century restoration. A description of the room exists in the time of the Fifth Duke in the letters of his sister-in-law, the Countess of Bessborough. To Lord Granville Leveson-Gower, in November 1797, she wrote:

I am sleeping in a black velvet room as large as the State rooms at Chatsworth, with the moon shining thro' the casement and making me see Ghosts and Goblins all round me. I really am half frighten'd, tho' I do not know very well at what. . . . [And in a second letter in the same vein] The little light there is can hardly find its way thro' Ivy and Iron bars that close my casement, and the wind whistles dolefully thro' the crevices and blows about the loose Arras. Nothing can be more gloomy, but yet I like it of all things.

With such a reaction it is no wonder that the Old English style became so popular within a few years, and that Robinson should have had the room engraved for *Vitruvius Britannicus.*

The watercolours of the Long Gallery by Hunt and Cox, the latter done in 1840, show the room after its restoration by the Sixth Duke. Walpole had been disappointed with the tapestries and pictures, and about 1790 some repairs were carried out and the 18th-century chairs sent from London. The re-hanging of the portraits was done for the Sixth Duke, who also sent more from Chatsworth, Chiswick and London to make a visually balanced set that played up the historical character of the room. In his *Handbook* he listed them, saying 'The pictures, of little value, separate, have become interesting as a series.' Much the finest of these was the Holbein cartoon of Henry VIII now in the National Portrait Gallery that can be seen in the window bay in Cox's watercolour. The Duke also sent from Chatsworth the canopy and back of the State Bed made for the First Duke by Lapierre, and had it placed halfway down the Gallery, where it remains. The result was, as Mark Girouard has described it, 'an effect of great, but mellow richness, and romantic light and shade'.

Hatfield House Hertfordshire

When Mme de Staël saw the house in 1813, she was delighted with 'the Feudal grandeur in the appearance of Hatfield, at its antiquity, and much pleas'd with all the tradition Lord Salisbury told her of Queen Elizabeth being confin'd there'. It was just the kind of house to appeal to the early 19th century, but it owes at least some of its existing Jacobean character to the restoration by the Second Marquess of Salisbury, the son of Mme de Staël's host, who inherited in 1823 and lived until 1868. Henry Shaw's view of the Gallery done for P. F. Robinson's *Vitruvius Britannicus* in 1833 shows it before Lord Salisbury embellished it after his second marriage in 1847. Robinson wrote of it: 'The general character of this Gallery corresponds in every respect with the antiquity of its architectural decoration: choice old Japan cabinets are interspersed with a collection of porcelain, numerous candelabra, and ancient chairs. . . .' In the recess on the right can be seen the Jacobean organ decorated by Rowland Bucket. The Second Marquess had evidently removed the more obviously 18th-century furniture and restored the Gallery character, and in this it offers an interesting comparison with what the Sixth Duke of Devonshire was doing in the Gallery at Chatsworth. Robinson also mentioned the *tableaux* of scenes from Sir Walter Scott's novels arranged in the Gallery early in 1833. They were designed by David Wilkie at the special request of the Duke of Wellington, and *The Times* correspondent wrote: 'The dresses of the

7

VAN DYKE ROOM AT HATFIELD HOUSE, HERTFORDSHIRE. *An anonymous watercolour, 1844.*

personages who figured in the *tableaux* were magnificent, but no sense but the *sight* was gratified. The niggardly supply of refreshments – there being nothing to eat or drink after the small allowance of tea and hot water was exhausted – made everybody discontented.' When Queen Victoria and Prince Albert visited Hatfield in 1846, the Gallery was used for a ball, but the occasion was not a success, because, as Lord David Cecil has written, 'Neither guest made a good impression on the company'. Later the Gallery became the main family sitting-room, a use that underlines the breakdown of the distinction between family and state rooms in many great houses in the course of the 19th century.

THE LONG GALLERY AT HARDWICK. *A watercolour by David Cox.*

MARY QUEEN OF SCOTS ROOM. *A watercolour by W. H. Hunt, 1828.*

Chatsworth, Derbyshire

William Hunt's watercolours done in 1822 and 1827 show the house in transition. Immediately after he inherited in 1811, the Sixth Duke of Devonshire had plunged into great activity at his many houses, and the view of the present Lower Library shows what were probably some of his early purchases; the glazed bookcase, the ormolu candelabra on the chimneypiece, and the white curtains, their valances trimmed with black. However, the architectural design of the room was not altered, and William Talman's characteristic broad pilasters designed for the First Duke are clearly visible. The simplicity of the room and use of white throughout did not appeal to the Duke in later years, as he explained in his *Handbook*, and in 1839 he had the room elaborately redecorated by Crace, only the wainscot and chimneypiece being retained. It was here that the Duke placed Bishop Dampier's library when he bought it in 1812, but soon the pressure of books forced him to undertake a more ambitious scheme, the conversion of the First Duke's Gallery into a Library. This had been the finest room in the Baroque house, with handsome pilasters and entablature framing painted panels, and with a ceiling by Goudge incorporating paintings by Verrio. In 1816, two years before he began his major alterations designed by Wyatville, the Duke had the painted panels taken down and the spaces between the pilasters made into bookcases. Over a decade later the room was remodelled again, with a gallery inserted to serve new bookcases running right round it, so that all that was left of the First Duke's scheme was the ceiling. Hunt's watercolour shows a pair of marble vases that were typical of the taste of the Sixth Duke, who became enamoured of the material and of sculpture in general during his visit to Rome in 1819. He also shows one of a pair of Kentian presses for folio books that are still in the library today.

8

THE LONG GALLERY AT HATFIELD. *Henry Shaw's engraving from* Vitruvius Britannicus, *1833.*

9

QUEEN VICTORIA AND GUESTS IN THE GALLERY. *An anonymous watercolour, 1846.*

10

THE GALLERY AT CHATSWORTH, DERBYSHIRE. *A watercolour by W. H. Hunt, 1827.*

Burghley House
Lincolnshire

12
THE STATE DRAWING ROOM AT BURGHLEY HOUSE, LINCOLNSHIRE. *An etching by Lady Sophia Cecil, 1817.*

There have been three great periods in the history of Burghley: the first its actual building between the 1550s and 80s by William Cecil, the First Lord Burghley; the second at the end of the 17th century when the Fifth Earl of Exeter remodelled the greater part of the interior; and a third under the Ninth Earl, who, having succeeded in 1754, more or less completed the Fifth Earl's work and largely refurnished the house. His successor, the First Marquess of Exeter, made certain changes in 1797 in anticipation of a visit from the Prince of Wales. It is thanks to his daughter, Lady Sophia Cecil (d. 1823), the wife of Henry-Manvers Pierrepont, that we have a record of the principal rooms about 1817–21, soon after her brother, the Second Marquess, came of age. Her rare etchings, clearly influenced by Thomas Hope's plates, can be related to descriptions of the house in guidebooks of 1815 and 1847.

Two of the plates show state rooms and the other three are of the private apartments on the ground floor. In the etchings it may not be clear that the decoration of the state rooms is of two dates, the painted ceilings by Verrio being of the Fifth Earl's time and the woodwork of the Ninth Earl's. Although the state rooms were not finally completed until the walls of the staircase were painted in the early 19th century, their layout follows Baroque practice; indeed the First Duke of Devonshire, the builder of Chatsworth, and the Fifth Earl were brothers-in-law. The State Drawing-Room, the third of the range of five rooms and generally now called the Third George Room, has changed remarkably little since Lady Sophia's day: the statues and the Medusa's head by Nollekens are still on the chimneypiece supplied by Bartoli, and the big flower pictures and the overmantel picture of St Gregory the Great by Sacchi have not been changed, nor have the corner cupboards of old floral marquetry made up by Ince and Mayhew in 1767–8. It is interesting to see how the floral motif was continued in the mid-18th-century chairs (now mainly in the State Bedroom). However, the uniformity of framing is partly artist's licence.

The Ninth Earl also put the Piranesi chimneypiece in the State Bedroom, now called the Second George Room but in fact the fourth room of the apartment working backwards from the staircase, as was the Fifth Earl's intention. The elaborate bed, together with its matching window curtains and draped valances, was ordered by his successor from Fell and Newton in 1797. A costly and extravagant affair, it was lavishly gilded and, according to a contemporary guidebook, it was hung with 250 yards of striped coral velvet of British manufacture and lined with 900 yards of white satin, the trimmings being coral coloured and the deep silk fringe black; unfortunately it was altered for Queen Victoria's visit in 1844.

Lady Sophia's etching of the South Dining-Room on the ground floor, which had evidently been used for that purpose at least since the second half of the 18th century, is interesting partly because she shows the layout of plate. The guidebook describes 'two magnificent sideboards, which contain a rich profusion of costly gilt coronation plate of large dimensions among which is the largest silver cistern in England. ... Upon the sideboards also are four large round dishes, being coronation plate, given to the family by King James II, Queen Anne, and George I, several large cups, and an Ewer. ...' It is remarkable that such a display was always set out for visitors. The existence of an 18th-century fireplace and the screen of columns suggest that the Ninth Earl may have enlarged the room, the earlier part of which dates from the Fifth Earl's time, having a fine contemporary ceiling and a richly carved overmantel. On the left of the etching appears an easy chair, evidently a not unusual introduction into early 19th-century dining-rooms and seen in several other illustrations.

On the far side of the Marble Hall lies the Red Drawing-Room, which in 1785 was 'the principal drawing-room, hung with crimson damask and ornamented with four capital pictures by Luca Giordano'. It too has a fine ceiling done about 1680, and over the chimneypiece Lady Sophia shows the magnificent frame carved by Ince and Mayhew in 1767–8 to take the largest piece of mirror glass hitherto made in England. Already the 18th-century formality still surviving in the state rooms upstairs had been broken up with two deep sofas (braided in a pseudo-military style deriving from France) flanking the fireplace, with tables of different forms in front of them. The armchair on the left, probably one of the set etched in the Third George Room but still downstairs in 1965, seems to have an antimacassar hanging down its back, an addition presumably made to protect the fine needlework upholstery. It is unusual to see the shovels and the bellows hanging from nails in the dado.

In the Blue Drawing-Room, which the 1847 guide described as the private sitting-room, or boudoir, of Lady Exeter, and hung with blue striped silk tabouret, can be seen some of the furniture supplied by Fell and Newton to the First Marquess. Their pier glasses with the cabinets for china but made as bookcases, and the overmantel mirror with the palm tree decorations, are still *in situ*, as is the Charles II ceiling and carving round the overmantel picture. The pelmet cornices were also part of Fell and Newton's order, and it is interesting to see that their festoon curtains had not been altered by 1821. Whether the cushions in the sofa and settee were really squared off is impossible to say, but Sheraton, Smith and Ackermann show them in a similar manner.

13 and 14
THE STATE BEDROOM AND THE RED DRAWING ROOM. *Etchings by Lady Sophia Cecil dated 1817 and 1821.*

15 and 16
THE BLUE DRAWING ROOM AND THE DINING ROOM. *Etchings by Lady Sophia Cecil dated 1821 and 1820.*

Petworth House, Sussex

Of all the pictures of English interiors, Turner's views of Petworth painted about 1828 while staying with his friend and patron, the Third Earl of Egremont, are the finest – indeed perhaps the only ones to be considered as works of art. So it is, of course, unfair to bracket them with the watercolours painted in the 1860s by Mrs Percy Wyndham, a daughter-in-law of Lord Leconfield and the wife of the builder of Clouds, Philip Webb's celebrated house in Wiltshire; but together they give a rare picture of a great house over a hundred years ago. The earliest interior to be recorded is the Marble Hall, the only important late 17th-century interior done for the Duke of Somerset to survive virtually unaltered. Next in time is the Rococo White and Gold Room painted by Turner in 1828; then comes Mrs Wyndham's view of the celebrated Carved Room formed by the Third Earl and arranged more or less as it is today; the Sculpture Gallery was also the work of the Third Earl about the same time, but Mrs Wyndham shows it after he had enlarged it in 1824; and last comes the Red (now called the White) Library.

The Third Earl (1751–1837) was a gifted, generous and unconventional man and, although less is known about him than is deserved, he is rightly remembered as a patron of British artists and their host in Sussex. Turner is the most famous of that company, but Phillips, Northcote, Constable, Leslie, Flaxman and Westmacott all had fruitful contact with him. His purchases of British sculpture complemented his father's interest in antique marbles, and it was to house the latter that he had first formed the Sculpture Gallery. Mrs Wyndham's watercolour shows the southward view with the original 17th-century arcade on the left and the big north bay added on in 1824. Recently the Gallery has been painted terracotta to approximate more closely to the dark Pompeian colour of the mid-19th century, the walls

being hung with many pictures by Lord Egremont's contemporaries.

One would not expect to look at a Turner for precise details, but in the White and Gold Room, which was decorated under the supervision of Matthew Brettingham the elder between 1754 and 1765, it is interesting to see crimson festoon curtains drawn up to the heads of the great windows looking out over the park.

Mrs Wyndham's watercolour of the Carved Room gives a sense of the rather different character of the house in the time of the Third Earl's son, George Wyndham – he did not inherit the earldom because his parents did not marry until after they had had six children, but he was created Lord Leconfield in 1859 – and she suggests a private version of *The Melton Breakfast* painted by Sir Francis Grant. How long it had been used as a dining room is not known, but when Lady Eastlake visited the house in 1850 she described it as the Chief Drawing Room. When the Third Earl created the room out of two smaller ones, the carving was rearranged and restored, but the result must have been rather overpowering, as the watercolour suggests, and some of the subsidiary panels or ornaments were removed later. The gilt tables still flank the fireplace.

The Marble Hall, so called on account of its black and white floor, was where the Third Earl had received the Allied Sovereigns in 1814, an event commemorated by Phillips, who shows Lord Egremont welcoming the Prince Regent, Tsar Alexander I, the Grand Duchess of Oldenburg, Frederick William III of Prussia and his son Frederick William IV, and the Prince of Württemberg. A generation later it had evidently become a writing- and music-room, with a big table before the fire and a piano, as well as the 18th-century chamber organ fitted behind a dummy door. For comfort a carpet covered the floor and, as was evidently not unusual, a drugget

lay along the main route across the room

By the 1860s Petworth had become a comfortable, relaxed Victorian house, and nowhere is this atmosphere more apparent than in the Red Library with its chintz covered chairs and sofas. It was the family sitting-room and evidently formed out of two rooms, a fault in the eyes of Salvin, who cut off the extension, originally the King of Spain's Bedchamber, shown in Mrs Wyndham's watercolour when he formed the White Library.

However, the house should really be remembered in the old Earl's time, as when Greville came in December 1832, the day after Lord Egremont's eightieth birthday.

He . . . hates ceremony, and can't bear to be personally meddled with; he likes people to come and go as it suits them, and say nothing about it, never to take leave of him. . . . Lord Egremont lives with an abundant though not very refined hospitality. The house wants modern comforts, and the servants are rustic and uncouth; but everything is good, and it bears an air of solid and aristocratic grandeur. . . .

18 and 19
THE WHITE AND GOLD ROOM AND THE RED LIBRARY. *Watercolours by J. M. W. Turner, about 1828.*

17
THE RED LIBRARY AT PETWORTH, SUSSEX. *A watercolour by Mrs Percy Wyndham, 1860s.*

38

Castle Howard Yorkshire

THE GALLERY

John Jackson's portrait of the Fifth Earl of Carlisle and his son, later the Dean of Lichfield, in the Gallery at Castle Howard marks the end of a building story stretching back over a hundred years. The Third Earl of Carlisle, who had embarked on the house in 1699, had not been able to make even a start on the West Wing, and it was only in the 1750s, in the time of the Fourth Earl, that the shell was built to the design of his brother-in-law, Sir Thomas Robinson, who abandoned Vanbrugh's conception. Then the Fourth Earl died in 1758, and, although the trustees of his ten-year-old son roofed the range, the interior was left and it was not until about 1800 that the Fifth Earl was in a sufficiently strong financial position to contemplate finishing it. He had become one of the most important collectors of his day, being one of the triumvirate who had acquired a stake in the Italian and Dutch portions of the Orleans collection, the other two being the Third

Duke of Bridgewater and the First Marquess of Stafford, his brother-in-law and father-in-law. It was to house part of his share of the collection and to complete his father's wing that he commissioned designs from C. H. Tatham, whom he had met in Rome. The work was actually done in two stages, the southern section in 1801–2 and the central Octagon and northern section in 1811–12. Tatham published the scheme in 1811, employing as his engraver Henry Moses, one of the most talented and influential illustrators of the day.

The original black and gold pelmet cornices remain, as do the red curtains trimmed with a black Greek key design, their valances knotted up at each end and finished off with a deep black knotted fringe, and the gilt metal chandeliers, the design of which Tatham published in 1806. It is interesting to compare the Egyptian character of the chimney-piece and the tables that flank it with the chimneypiece and tables in Nash's Gallery at Attingham (Plate 97). Fine neo-classical frames of the same pattern as those flanking the draped arch still exist round some of the portraits in the Gallery. The picture, which is undated, but probably painted about 1812, shows the view from the South Gallery across the Octagon to the North Gallery.

24
THE FIFTH EARL OF CARLISLE AND ON[E] OF HIS SONS IN THE GALLERY AT CASTL[E] HOWARD, YORKSHIRE. *Painted by Joh[n] Jackson about 1810.*

THE NORTH END OF THE GALLERY.

26 and 27

THE CHIMNEY AND WINDOW WALLS OF
THE SOUTHERN SECTION OF THE
GALLERY. *Plates 25–27 are of Henry Moses's
engravings from C. H. Tatham's* The Gallery at
Castle Howard *(1811).*

Woburn Abbey
Bedfordshire

The Library at Woburn appears to be the only room of which there are three views (not including photographs) done at different times in the 19th century, and they show changing habits in furniture arrangement. The history of the room began with the Fifth Duke of Bedford, who, having inherited at the age of five in 1771, returned from the Grand Tour in 1786 to enter the Whig circle that revolved round the Prince of Wales and frequented Brooks's Club designed ten years earlier by the Prince's favoured architect, Henry Holland. Not surprisingly the young Duke consulted Holland about Woburn, and between 1788 and 1790 they arranged new private apartments (now demolished) linking on to the libraries in the south front. Lady Bessborough, who stayed in 1797, wrote to Lord Granville Leveson-Gower: 'I never saw so delightful a room as the library here; it is very large, all the finest Editions magnificently bound. Over the bookcases some very fine pictures (portraits) most of them Titians, Rembrandts, etc., three great looking glasses, all the ornaments white and golden, and the furniture blue leather.'

Apart from Holland's own designs and detailed drawings by C. H. Tatham, who was then in his office, the earliest view is that drawn by J. G. Jackson and engraved by Henry Moses, published in 1827 as part of P. F. Robinson's *Vitruvius Britannicus*. The

chandelier, probably designed by Holland about 1790, is still there, as are the pelmet cornices. The ingenious book table on the right of the plate is now in the Gallery: probably designed by Holland about 1795, it consists of three upright bays to take very large books and has an attached reading table, shown in the plate with one of a pair of chairs by Jacob in front. The press with a sloping top on the left was also probably designed by Holland at the same time. A small but significant detail is the presence of the heating grills cut in the floors in the reveals of the windows. Doubtless Holland would have envisaged a formal arrangement of the furniture, but this had been modified by Robinson's day, and the upholstery changed from blue leather to green silk, and, although it was one of the rooms 'usually shown to strangers', he described how 'everything is princely, yet everything is full of comfort, and they are all kept in constant use as living rooms'. The latter aspect is admirably conveyed by the anonymous watercolour of about 1850, which shows groups of people in both libraries.

On the unexpected death of the Fifth Duke in 1802, he was succeeded by his brother whose principal contribution to Woburn was to complete the transformation of Henry Holland's Greenhouse into a Sculpture Gallery. This had been begun by the

28
THE LIBRARY AT WOBURN ABBEY, BEDFORDSHIRE. *Henry Moses's engraving for* Vitruvius Britannicus *(1827) based on a drawing by J. G. Jackson.*

29 and 30

THE LIBRARY. An anonymous watercolour about 1850 and a painting by Lady Ela Russell, 1884.

Fifth Duke the year before he died, and it was he who had commissioned Holland to design the Temple of Liberty (seen at the far end of the *Vitruvius Britannicus* plate) dedicated to his Whig heroes. In 1815 the Sixth Duke acquired four marble columns, and it was to incorporate them in the centre of the gallery that Wyatville constructed the screens that year. As well as collecting antiquities the Sixth Duke was a great patron of leading contemporary sculptors, in particular Canova, Thorvaldsen and Chantrey, and in this he had a considerable influence on the aims of the young Sixth Duke of Devonshire. The sculp-

ture remained *in situ* in the Gallery until recent years, a remarkable expression of late Regency taste.

The Sixth Duke died in 1861 and the third picture of the Library was painted by Lady Ela Sackville Russell in 1884, in the time of her father, the Ninth Duke. This shows the book table still beside the windows and what could be one of the chairs in a loose cover on the right. The two armchairs appear to be Victorian and not part of the splendid set of French gilt chairs that now furnishes the rooms.

THE SCULPTURE GALLERY AT WOBURN.
Henry Moses's engraving for Vitruvius Britannicus *based on a drawing by J. G. Jackson.*

32

THE GOTHICK HALL AT WELBECK ABBEY,
NOTTINGHAMSHIRE. *An etching by Lady
Sophia Cecil.*

Welbeck Abbey
Nottinghamshire

THE GOTHICK HALL

Lady Sophia Cecil's etching, dated 1821, shows the Gothick Hall originally fitted up by the Countess of Oxford and not very carefully adapted as a Library by the Third Duke of Portland, who died in 1809. During the 1740s, after her husband's death, Lady Oxford, who had inherited Welbeck from her father, the First Duke of Newcastle, made many changes in the house, the most important being the creation of this room, one of the earliest ambitious interiors in the Gothick taste and ante-dating the main rooms at both Arbury and Strawberry Hill. The designer is not certain, but work was evidently begun in about 1746 (the year before Batty Langley's *Gothic Architecture* was published), and the room was finished after 1750. On Lady Oxford's death in 1755, Welbeck passed to her daughter, the wife of the Second Duke of Portland, and it was with her that Mrs Delany stayed in 1756. Mrs Delany considered that 'for workmanship in the true Gothick taste . . . the Great Hall exceeds everything I have seen of the kind'. However, succeeding generations disapproved of Lady Oxford's

Gothick rooms, and Repton thought that the Hall was the only one worth keeping. Today all that survives of it is the elaborate fan vault and the lower half of the chimneypiece. A piece of Lady Oxford's Gothick furniture can be seen in Plate 172.

Stowe, Buckinghamshire

THE DUCHESS'S DRAWING ROOM

This watercolour in the style of Joseph Nash shows one of the finest rooms at Stowe, after 1838 and a few years before the great sale of 1848. The room had been formed as the State Bedchamber for Earl Temple in the 1750s, the decoration designed by Giambattista Borra being completed in 1755, except for the Star and Collar of the Garter added in 1760. The State Bed stood in the recess at the far end until shortly before the visit of Queen Victoria in 1845, when the room became the Duchess's Drawing Room. The First Duke of Buckingham, who died in 1839, had acquired many treasures for Stowe as well as inheriting others through his wife, the daughter of the last Duke of Chandos, and, until he was forced to sell many of the pictures in 1834, the interior of the house saw its finest period. The Second Duke also added to the contents, but, according to a full contemporary description, spoilt its character. The watercolour certainly shows a very richly furnished room but one not over-furnished by the standards of the day. The very fine carpet with its display of arms survived the 1848 sale and remained until the final sale of 1921. The appliqué with shield-shaped glass to the left of the lacquer cabinet is one of a set that has survived. The plates in the recess by the window are part of a collection of more than 160 pieces of majolica.

33
THE DUCHESS'S DRAWING ROOM AT STOWE, BUCKINGHAMSHIRE. *Watercolour by or in the manner of Joseph Nash about 1845.*

Cassiobury Park Hertfordshire

THE GREAT LIBRARY

John Britton's book on Cassiobury (1837), from which this plate of the library comes, was inspired by other similar recent books, among them Buckler's *Eaton Hall* (1826) and Lord Braybrooke's *History of Audley End* (1836), but its illustrations were a miscellaneous series that had been given to Britton by the owner of the house, the Fifth Earl of Essex, a generous patron of contemporary artists including Turner as a young man. After he succeeded in 1799 Lord Essex had employed James Wyatt to recast the Charles II house in the Gothick style but retaining some Restoration features, including the splendid staircase now in the Metropolitan Museum, New York. Prince Puckler-Muskau, who went there in 1826, described how 'You enter a hall with coloured windows, which afford a view into an inner court laid out as a flower-garden: leaving the hall, you go through a long gallery on the side, hung with armour, to the rich carved oak staircase leading to the library, which here generally serves as principal drawing room.' It is this room that the elder Pugin drew; it was one of four devoted to books, and contained those on classics, history, travel and philosophy. Over the bookcases were fifteen family pictures with Reynolds's portrait of Lord Essex and his sister at the age of ten in the place of honour over the fireplace, and framed in rich carving by Grinling Gibbons. The windows have elaborate valances evidently trimmed with contrasting braid and deep fringe, but it is suprising to see what would now be regarded

34
THE GREAT LIBRARY AT CASSIOBURY, HERTFORDSHIRE. *An aquatint by F. Lewis based on a drawing by Augustus Pugin published by John Britton, 1837.*

as a hall lantern complete with its glass shade hanging on a counter weight in the centre of the room. The arrangement of the L-shaped settees and armchairs round the fire and the placing of the sofa table and reading chair is relaxed and comfortable, and there is a strong sense of the variety of occupations expected – reading, writing, and looking at prints all being planned for.

Eaton Hall, Cheshire

When the Second Earl Grosvenor, who succeeded in 1802, was planning to rebuild Eaton Hall, William Porden, his architect, championed the Gothick style on the grounds of 'preserving that distinction to Rank and Fortune, which it is the habit of the age to diminish . . . with regard to splendour it is far superior, and its variety is infinite'. Porden always had a high idea of his patron's position, even if he lectured him about it, and he spent a corresponding amount of his money on expressing it (over £100,000 by 1812). The result was that Eaton Hall became one of the most extravagant Gothick houses built in the first quarter of the 19th century, the first phase being carried out between 1803 and 1812 and the second in 1820–6. In 1824, before the second phase was finished, John Buckler visited the house and two years later published his *Views of Eaton Hall in Cheshire*. Needless to say, thirteen-year-old Princess Victoria was very impressed when she visited it in 1832, but others had different views. Prince Puckler-Muskau, for instance, who visited it in 1827, found

the house excited just the same feeling in me as Ashridge, only with the difference that it is still more over-loaded, and internally far less beautiful, although furnished still more expensively, in parts. . . . In this chaos of modern gothic excrescences, I remarked ill-painted modern glass windows, and shapeless tables and chairs, which most incongruously affected to imitate architectural ornaments. . . . Treasures of art I saw none; the best was a middling picture by West. All the magnificence lay in the gorgeous materials, and the profuse display of money.

Indeed it was not even comfortable. In 1826 Lord Grosvenor's daughter-in-law, Lady Belgrave, wrote: 'We are in the most serious difficulty about water. All the pipes in the brewery, laundry etc., are all frozen up, not to mention those in the apartments. It is a great trouble, as a good many people are coming tomorrow and what is to be done we know not!' And several years later she found the place as 'cold and comfortless as usual'.

The plan of the house followed that of its Charles II predecessor on the site, with a Hall and Saloon on axis, even part of the Caroline ceiling of the old Saloon being incorporated in the new one. It was at Lord Grosvenor's insistence that the Saloon was decorated all in blue, but there had been a struggle with Porden over this, the architect finally saying: 'I therefore think your Lordship might venture to retain blue furniture in the Saloon, for at the most it will be only a single sacrifice of painting to upholstery.' From the beginning Porden had set a great store by the stained glass, saying 'the Saloon may be fitted up to have solemnity or cheerfulness as more or less painted glass is introduced', and in 1808 he recommended it to be 'as brilliant with stained glass as possible'. However, care was taken not to obscure the view across the Cheshire plain to the rock with the ruins of Beeston Castle and the Peckforton Hills. Little Regency stained glass survives in houses today, but its popularity can be gathered from its frequent appearance in the illustrations in this book.

35

THE DINING ROOM AT EATON HALL, CHESHIRE. *Plates 35–37 are Buckler watercolours of 1824 prepared for* Views of Eaton Hall (1826).

36
THE LIBRARY AT EATON HALL

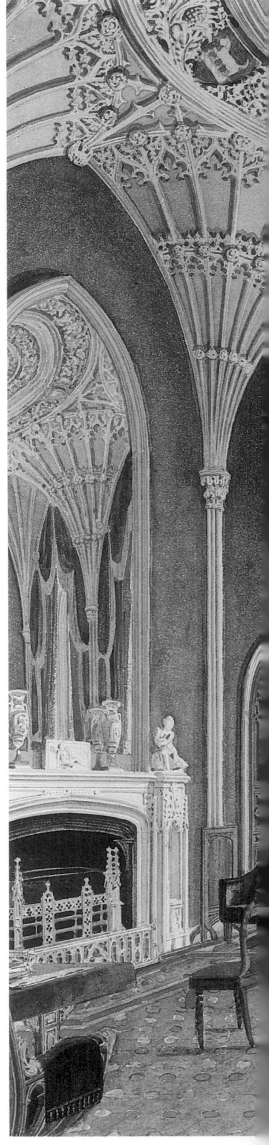

The furniture was evidently all supplied by Gillows and apart from the Gothic armchairs now at Basildon Park, Berkshire, there were lighter, parlour chairs of two patterns and another pattern of armchairs beside one of the two firescreens. Next to the armchair appears a Grecian couch with crimson upholstery, and in front of it a table with a cloth over it, the same arrangement being repeated on the far side of the fireplace. The elaborate curtains were presumably draped by Joseph Kay, Porden's son-in-law, whom he said 'understands them both as a Painter and an Upholsterer'. The appearance of the Grosvenor arms as the central feature of the valance to the central window recalls the early 19th-century valance in the Dining Room at Shugborough. The carpets in the principal rooms were done to an overall pattern but in different colourings, consisting of medallion designs and elaborate Gothic borders, each one having its hearth rug.

The Dining Room, presumably depicted about breakfast-time, was also one of Porden's early rooms. Its walls and curtains were scarlet, while the Gothic vault had a pale blue wash. The amount of stained glass was reduced because 'the Dresses of your Society in times of Gala would suffer like statues and pictures'. On the other hand the mirrored sideboard was intended to 'reflect and multiply the plate and lustres upon it'. The centre

of the carpet was shown covered with a plain drugget. Sometimes, as here, this was laid to protect the carpet, but Ackermann in 1809 recommended 'crimson drugget, milled to a proper substance, and panelled with a border of black furniture cloth [as] producing a warm and rich appearance' and so suitable for dining-rooms. The chairs have disappeared, but a variant classical pattern exists at Attingham Park, Shropshire: between the top of the back and the upholstery was a panel of stamped brass.

The Library was shown virtually unfurnished, but possibly it was not finished in 1824. Succeeding Grosvenors were constantly altering the house, major modifications being done by Burn in 1846 and then a complete remodelling in a different Gothic style by Waterhouse in the 1870s. Now Porden's house appears as a Gothick Brighton Pavilion, but it is also worth remembering the family point of view expressed by Harriet, Countess Gower: 'They must feel it a relief to be out of the eternal gothic of Eaton.'

37
THE SALOON.

48

Audley End, Essex

A large set of watercolours of both the exterior and the interior in 1853 during the time of the Third Lord Braybrooke can be related to a description of it in 1847 by Mrs George Bancroft, the wife of the American minister. The great Jacobean house, reduced by Vanbrugh in 1721 and altered for the First Lord Braybrooke mainly by Adam, had been extensively altered and restored by the Third Lord Braybrooke (best known for his edition of Pepys's *Diary*) in the years immediately after he inherited in 1825, to make it more convenient for entertaining on a large scale, and to emphasize its historic character. His main change had been to create reception rooms on the level of the Saloon, on the first floor, and to convert Robert Adam's two drawing rooms on the ground floor into a State Bedroom and dressing-room. It was here that Mrs Bancroft was put up 'in the state bed of blue and gold',

38, 39 and 40
THE SALOON, STATE BEDROOM AND STATE DRESSING ROOM AT AUDLEY END, ESSEX. *Plates 38–42 are unsigned watercolours of 1853.*

the walls being hung with the original crimson and white damask and lots of pictures: 'among others a full length of Queen Charlotte, just opposite the foot of the bed, always saluted me every morning when I awoke, with her fan, her hoop, and her deep ruffles'. In the 1853 watercolour the carpet is drawn to one side so that between the doors in use are just bare boards; upstairs in the Gallery a drugget was laid across the carpets to save them. Outside the Gallery door can be seen a large cast-iron radiator, and also part of the large collection of stuffed birds formed by the Fourth Lord Braybrooke, both still there today.

Not only are the state and reception-rooms recorded but some of the family rooms, including Lady Braybrooke's Sitting Room, which was evidently her dressing-room, hung with a crisp gay chintz, and the schoolroom and nursery. Whoever did the drawings knew the house very well, and it has been suggested that they may be by Lord Braybrooke's sister-in-law, Charlotte Neville-Grenville, whose husband retired as Master of Magdalene College, Cambridge, that year.

41 and 42   THE GALLERY AND SCHOOLROOM.

Mount Edgcumbe, Cornwall

THE HALL

The contrast between the Hall at Mount Edgcumbe and the views of Cotehele that follow is intentional, because it helps to explain why Cotehele survived, the family preferring Mount Edgcumbe with its superb site running down to Plymouth harbour. Despite the Georgian appearance of the Hall, it was the central Great Hall of the 16th-century house and rose up in a way similar to that at Wollaton. The classicizing was probably done by one of Reynolds's early local patrons, the First Lord Mount Edgcumbe, who was ennobled in 1742. According to the 1821 guidebook, which was principally concerned with the grounds, 'the interior contains nothing very remarkable except the hall in the centre, which was originally Gothic . . . ;' but it goes on to say that it was occasionally used as a summer dining room and was very good for music.

The Hall was destroyed when the house was burnt in the Second World War.

43

THE HALL AT MOUNT EDGCUMBE, CORNWALL. *An anonymous early 19th-century painting.*

Cotehele, Cornwall

The influence of Nash's *Mansions*, the first volume of which appeared in 1838, is apparent in the Rev F. V. J. Arundell's *History of Cotehele* (c. 1840) with its coloured lithographic plates by Nicholas Condy, a local artist. It is the romantic aspects of the medieval house that come through most strongly, and that is right, because by then it had become a well-known place of pilgrimage. King George III and Queen Charlotte went to see it in 1789; and Harriet, Countess Granville, the Sixth Duke of Devonshire's sister, wrote an account of her visit there in 1815 that still seems topical:

First Lady Boringdon [her hostess at Saltram], with an old green shawl swinging over her shoulders, the corners all wrong, her hair about her ears, a cap just sticking on to the back of her head and her hat in her hand, shouting out to the housekeeper to be in readiness for us. No wonder that a maid who first appeared told her she must not *presume* to come in. Lord Lansdowne, very fat and out of breath in a black chip hat much *enforcé* over his head. Lady Cowper swinging after them, her nose very red, a high hat tied on with a veil under her chin, flounces draggling, sash untying, shawl floating . . . we lead the life of tourists, have delicious weather, little repose and no time.

Twelve years later Lady Georgiana Agar-Ellis was taken there by Lord Valletort, the son of the Second Earl of Mount Edgcumbe, and they had dinner in 'that delightful old dining room. . . . One really felt transposed to the times in which the house was built; everything in such perfect keeping and character, the old pewter plates, with family arms, the tall, narrow wine glasses, the salt cellars, spoons, forks, tankards, salvers, etc., all in complete union.'

Arundell's style was purple and with Shaw's book on furniture being comparatively recent, he did not fully understand the contents of the house. For instance he wrote that

all the rooms retain their ancient furniture, and the latest is not more modern than the reign of Elizabeth! What an exquisite feast for the antiquary, and not less so to every one possessing the slightest longing for an insight into the ancient mansion of an old English Knight! – to see him in his banqueting hall – in his private chapel – in his family apartments, etc., to see the armour worn by him and his retainers – the board at which he feasted – the chairs on which he sat – the bed on which he lay – the tapestry covering his walls, and even the most minute details of his domestic menage.

To what extent they were rearranged for picturesque effect or even added to is impossible to ascertain, but, according to the Rev. Thomas Talbot's description of a visit in 1811, the place sends 'one in imagination four centuries back . . . the Beds, Cabinets and all the furniture is of the same period; what few things are not originally belonging to the House having been carefully adapted to the style and date of the whole'. Who was responsible for this adaptation is not clear. It could have been George, First Earl of Mount Edgcumbe, who became an FSA in 1792, but as he died in 1795 it seems more likely that it was done by the Second Earl, making it more or less contemporary with Browsholme. Certainly the arrangement of the Great Hall existed in more or less its present form by the time Buckler did a watercolour of it in 1812. Although by then the house had become primarily a place to visit, the family continued to stay there once a year 'with as large a party as the House will hold and they are served on the old Pewter and live as nearly as possible in the old manner.' Condy's view of Sir Piers Edgcumbe's early 16th-century Great Hall depicts 'the refreshing sight of the good domestics of the present noble possessors of Cotehele, in full activity of preparation for the annual banquet to all his tenantry'.

The tapestry-hung rooms are a reminder that the house is still very rich in materials of different dates as well as furniture, some of it almost as early as Arundell thought but most of it dating from the 17th and early 18th centuries. On the bed in the Best Bedroom for instance, Condy depicted 'an ancient altar cloth, formed of red velvet, powdered with fleur-de-lis', and, with an eye on current fashions, Arundell wrote of ebony chairs and a sofa in the Drawing Room that they 'immediately attract the eye, as they would the heart of many a curiosity dealer in Wardour Street, where now and then an ebony

air of much inferior workmanship may be seen at the prohibiting price of from fifteen to twenty pounds'. The beds are particularly interesting: that in the South Room has hangings of linen embroidered with red wool made about 1680; in the King Charles Room the made-up bed has 17th-century needlework applied to its hangings.

In certain details like the pots on the floor in the Dining Room Condy was no doubt making an arrangement for picturesque effect rather as a photographer would today, but the table was set for receiving someone like Lady Georgiana Agar-Ellis and the general appearance and mood of his plates is still recognizable today. Cotehele remains one of the very few houses where time has indeed stood still.

44

PREPARATIONS FOR A TENANTS' DINNER IN THE GREAT HALL AT COTEHELE, CORNWALL. *Plates 44–48 are lithographs after watercolours by Nicholas Condy from Arundell's* History of Cotehele, *about 1840.*

45 and 46   THE PUNCH ROOM AND THE OLD DINING ROOM.

7 and 48   THE SOUTH ROOM AND KING CHARLES'S ROOM.

Baddesley Clinton
Warwickshire

THE HALL

The ancient moated house which the Ferrers family had acquired by marriage in the early 16th century was just the kind of house that appealed most to Victorian Romantic taste, but Mrs Ferrers's watercolour of the Hall, painted about 1870, is more than a record of a room; it is a reminder of a singularly touching story. Seated by the fire is her husband, whom she married in 1867, and on the far side of it her aunt, Georgiana, with whom she had lived after the death of her parents and who had married as her second husband Edward Heneage Dering, the fourth figure in the picture. Shortly after the Ferrerses married, the Derings came to stay at Baddesley Clinton and they were so moved by the old house that Mr Dering paid off the mortgages on the estate and gave the money needed to repair the house; and he and his wife came to live permanently with the Ferrerses. It was an idyll that lasted until the death of Mrs Dering in 1876. Then Mr Ferrers died in 1884, and finally after that Mr Dering married Mrs Ferrers.

The Old English character of the room is slightly misleading in that it may not be even on the same site as the medieval hall, and it was altered very considerably after Edward Ferrers's changes to the house in the time of Charles I. It was he who had originally set up the stone chimneypiece in the Great Chamber in the gatehouse, but it was brought

49

THE GREAT HALL AT BADDESLE CLINTON, WARWICKSHIRE. *A watercolou by Mrs Ferrers, about 1870.*

down to the Hall in 1737 by Thomas Ferrer who also seems to have altered the ceilin, The latter's very conservative treatment the room and the presence of the long ear 17th-century table at the left and the oa chests and chests of drawers suggest that i character may have antedated the influence the Picturesque and the enthusiasm for th Old English style.

Adare Manor, Co. Limerick, Eire

An early 19th-century watercolour of the Drawing-Room in the 18th-century house and a mid-19th-century drawing of the new Great Hall in its successor are admirable illustrations of the increase in scale of country house life in the first half of the last century, greater means being matched by grander ambitions and Romantic ideals. The water-colour of the drawing room shows the family of the Second Earl of Dunraven, who succeeded in 1824. In 1810 he had married a Gloucestershire heiress, Caroline Wyndham, and together in 1832 they embarked on the Romantic house that exists today. Pictures like the Panini, shown over the Drawing Room chimneypiece, were retained, but their ideas on planning can never have been comfortable in the Irish climate. The Great Hall, which is 53 feet long, 37 wide and 30 feet high, is linked to the Long Gallery on the first floor, which is 132 feet long, and they are only separated by an elaborately carved pierced door that could exclude no draughts. The Third Earl, who succeeded in 1850, eventually completed the house in the 1860s, having had the aid of Pugin in the design of the chimneypiece and staircase in the Great Hall. It is his children that are shown playing battledore and shuttlecock. Round them are suits of armour, a massive chair of bog oak, now in the Entrance Hall, and horns of the Irish elk. Lady Dunraven, the wife of the Second Earl and the author of *Memorials of Adare Manor*, described the room as 'peculiarly adapted to every purpose for which it may be required' and enjoyed 'the delicious tones' of the organ drifting into the Gallery.

50
THE DRAWING ROOM IN THE OLD HOUSE AT ADARE, CO LIMERICK. *An anonymous early 19th-century watercolour.*

51
THE GREAT HALL IN THE NEW HOUSE AT ADARE. *An anonymous drawing of the 1850s.*

Vinters, Kent

The Hall and the Drawing-Room at Vinters, near Maidstone in Kent, are interiors in a somewhat smaller house than most of those illustrated, but Charlotte Bosanquet's water-colours painted in 1843 are of particular interest, because they show the home of Susannah Whatman, whose *Housekeeping Book* of the 1770s was published in 1956. Mrs Whatman was one of the sisters of Charlotte Bosanquet's father and in 1776 she married James Whatman of Turkey Court. His business as a papermaker prospered and in 1782 he was able to buy the adjoining property of Vinters and remodel it in the Wyatt style. Although the latter was not the house in his wife's notes, Charlotte Bosanquet's water-colours add a dimension to the unique insight into Georgian life provided by Susannah Whatman's notes, into the way a well-to-do woman organized her household and instructed her servants as well as revealing what she expected to do herself. When Charlotte Bosanquet went to Vinters, it belonged to James Whatman's son by his first marriage, but it seems that little had changed in the previous fifty-five years, much of the furniture clearly having been acquired by his father. The sparseness of the hall with its pale green walls toning with the scagliola columns, its uncovered floor and its characteristic chairs is expected, but the mats before the doors are the kind of simple details that are normally taken for granted and never described.

Despite the books on the round table in the

52
THE HALL AT VINTERS, KENT. *Plates 52–54 are watercolours by Charlotte Bosanquet, about 1840.*

Drawing Room it looks a little-used room, and there is a sense of unease about the way the settees and chairs, which were probably in the French taste, are shown drawn into the room according to 19th-century practice. However, they are carefully protected by their striped covers. The strip carpet was probably of a more recent vintage than the chairs and it is seen covering the floor of the adjoining Library, which must have been the usual family sitting-room. The big round table in the centre was evidently almost *de rigeur* at that time, because it appears in so many views. More of Charlotte Bosanquet's watercolours are illustrated in Figs 125, 146-149.

53 and 54
THE DRAWING ROOM AND LIBRARY

Longford Hall
Shropshire

There are a number of country houses in Britain built by men who had spent their working lives in the service of the East India Company and who, having built up a fortune, returned hoping to establish a landed family. Ralph Leeke was one such man. Born in 1754, he went out to India when he was sixteen or seventeen and remained there until 1785, finding the Longford property near Newport on his return. He began the house in 1789, employing Joseph Bonomi as his architect, and he bought most of the furniture from Henry Kettle and Charles Elliott. Much of this remained at Longford until his descendants sold the house in the 1930s. Apparently the only record of its interiors before the sale are a series of watercolours by Lady Hester Leeke (1822–87), who had married his grandson in 1847. One of her exteriors is dated 1857, and so presumably it is safe to date the interiors to about 1855. By then a certain amount of Victorian upholstery and furniture had become mixed with the original furniture of the 1790s. In the Dining Room the carpet looks like a Turkey, which is what Ralph Leeke had ordered from Kettle's, and the red curtains may have been the original moreen, a woollen material thought very suitable for such a room. Beside the armchair at the end of the table appears a three-tier dumb waiter and round the room is a full complement of serving tables. The high chair suggests that a child was sometimes allowed to eat with the parents rather than always in the nursery.

Apart from recording the Drawing Room which had a very fine French wallpaper of which fragments survive in the Victoria and Albert Museum, Lady Hester painted the Hall and the Breakfast Room. More of her watercolours are illustrated in Plates 57 and 96 and 97

55 and 56
THE DINING ROOM AND MORNING ROOM AT LONGFORD HALL, SHROPSHIRE. *Plates 55–57 are watercolours by Lady Hester Leeke about 1855.*

Eridge Castle, Kent

THE DRAWING ROOM

Eridge Castle was one of the more extensive and less substantial Picturesque remodellings of an earlier house, and until its classicizing in 1938 was largely the work of the Second Earl of Abergavenny between 1790 and 1830. His forbears had given up living there at the end of the 17th century, preferring Kidbrook in Sussex. However, he decided to return to their ancient seat and emphasize the family history through the choice of architectural style. Thus, to a contemporary writer, 'The castle, as a dwelling, may be said to be possessed of much elasticity in its construction; it is calculated to hold a very large establishment; and it is a place at the same time, in its arrangement of its apartments, well adapted to afford great domestic comfort to a more limited family.' When the Second Earl died in 1843 he was succeeded by two of his sons in succession, both parsons. The Fourth Earl, who succeeded his brother in 1845, married Caroline Leeke, a daughter of Ralph Leeke of Longford, and it is this connection that explains the appearance of the Eridge Drawing Room in Lady Hester Leeke's album. Most of the interiors were Gothick to match the castellated exterior, but the Wyattesque Drawing Room in the centre of the first floor of the south front was evidently part of the

57

THE DRAWING ROOM AT ERIDGE CASTLE, KENT.

first phase of work, about 1790. The continued drapery and the furniture is Regency in character, but the lively red walls suggest that their colour may have been a later alteration. The way the curtains are drawn back to clear the windows and to drape across the oval mirrors is unusual. Although the fire is lit, a lady in black is seated protected by a screen. The absence of candles from the chandelier is a reminder of the reliance on portable lamps.

Knowle Cottage
Sidmouth, Devon

THE DRAWING ROOM

This plate from a rare book that described
Thomas L. Fish's marine villa is part of an
enchanting monument to vanity. The original
thatched *cottage ornée* had been built in 1805
by Lord Le Despencer, better known as Sir
Francis Dashwood of the Hell Fire Club, who
had devoted many years to the embellishment of his seat at West Wycombe; and it
had been greatly enlarged by Fish, who had
formed a Grand Suite of Rooms 100 feet in
length after he acquired the lease in 1820. By
1834, when the book came out, the house
must have been a literal folly, but the treatment of the interior and particularly the
Drawing Room, was evidently very decorative. The ground colours of the curtains and
carpet were carefully related, and both con-
trasted with the wallpaper below the pelmet
cornice. The trellis on the main walls and
ceiling may also have been a paper, possibly
having a cut-out border to outline the pelmet
cornice and two more rows to emphasize the
function of walls and ceiling. This decoration
recalls a now destroyed scheme carried out by
Morant about 1810.

58
THE VIEW FROM THE DRAWING ROOM A
KNOWLE COTTAGE, SIDMOUTH, DEVON
A plate from Guide to Illustrations of Knowl
Cottage *by C. F. Williams (1834).*

Luscombe Castle, Devon

THE DRAWING ROOM

In 1798 Charles Hoare, a partner in the family bank and a younger brother of Sir Richard Colt Hoare of Stourhead, began a castellated house near Dawlish for his delicate wife. The result was one of the most successful results of the partnership of John Nash and Humphry Repton, and fortunately the house remains much as it was in Charles Hoare's day. It is thought that the watercolour of the Drawing Room was done by Mrs Hoare about 1825, a few years after the room had been extended to the south. Only some of the painted decoration exists now, and the

'reliefs' over the bookcases, which may have been of paper like those in the Drawing Room at Caledon, have gone; so have some of the upper bookshelves in the recesses, the sky painting of the ceiling and the upper lights of stained glass. However, the Vulliamy clock on its original pedestal, on the left of the drawing, the chairs in the Egyptian taste made by the younger Chippendale, who also worked at Stourhead, and the round table that goes with them are still in there, as are the pelmet cornices. The combination of the carpet planned to the room, the solid

59
THE DRAWING ROOM AT LUSCOMBE, DEVON. *A watercolour thought to be by Mrs Hoare, about 1825.*

blocks of books, and the curtains with their deep pleated valances must have given the room a more solid impression than is apparent in modern photographs, and once again it illustrates the early 19th-century taste for a sitting-room-cum-library rather than a formal drawing room.

Saltram, Devon

THE LIBRARY

One of the rewards of searching for records of interiors is the way they reveal surprising continuity in the details of rooms. The conversation piece of the family in the Library at Saltram, for instance, shows the clock on the chimneypiece as having been there 150 years ago (when it had a dome), and the ormolu candelabra that flank it have only become exchanged with the pair on the other chimneypiece. The Library was the only important room in the house to be redecorated in the early 19th century, and was formed for the first Earl of Morley out of the old music room and library by John Foulston, the Plymouth architect, in 1818–19. In Nicholas Condy's picture Lord Morley can be seen on the left, and his illegitimate son Augustus Stapleton next to him, with Catchpole the butler standing up; Frances, Lady Morley, is seated at the table and beside her is her son Lord Boringdon. The picture is thought to have been painted in 1825, the year of Augustus

Stapleton's marriage. The screen of scagliola columns marks the division between the two old rooms. Over the bookcases can be seen part of the series of portraits of friends of Lord Morley's father, and Robert Adam's patron at Saltram, some by Reynolds and Northcote and no fewer than nine by Gilbert Stuart. The pier glasses are still in position,

60
THE LIBRARY AT SALTRAM, DEVON. *A painting by Nicholas Condy, about 1825.*

but the hanging lights have disappeared and so have the curtains with their draped valances.

61 and 62
THE DRAWING ROOM AND THE HALL
AND STAIRCASE AT WOOLLEY HALL,
YORKSHIRE. *One of Agostino Aglio's litho-
graphs of the house published in 1821.*

Woolley Hall, Yorkshire

In 1821 Agostino Aglio published a series of lithographs of the house in book form, dedicating them to Godfrey Wentworth Jnr, the son of his patron there. Aglio, who was born in Cremona in 1777, had settled in England early in the 19th century and worked principally as a theatrical decorator. Today the only major surviving scheme attributed to him is the ruin pieces on the staircase at Bretton Hall, Yorkshire, not far from Woolley. Aglio first worked at Woolley for Godfrey Wentworth in 1815 and in 1818 he returned to decorate a temporary ballroom for the com-

ing of age of Wentworth's son. In his book he included plates of the new entrance hall and staircase fitted out after a fire in 1796, the temporary Ballroom and, most important of all, the Drawing Room. This he had painted as a continuous landscape in the tradition of the Drakelow Hall room in the Victoria and Albert Museum and the painted room at Norbury Park, but defined by the architecture. The scheme also recalls the contemporary fashion for French landscape wallpaper. Unfortunately it no longer exists.

Guy's Cliffe, Warwickshire

THE DRAWING ROOM

Today the house is a pathetic ruin, but about 1860, when this watercolour was done, it belonged to the Hon. Charles Bertie-Greathead-Percy. The house had been inherited by his wife, whose forbear Samuel Greathead had built the mid-18th-century part. This was enlarged by Samuel Greathead's son about 1818 and then again about 1870 by the Percys, who had inherited it in about 1826, four years after their marriage. The building history is confused, but the Drawing Room as painted can be compared with the description of Prince Puckler-Muskau thirty-five years earlier:

"The whole is extremely picturesque, and the interior is fitted up with equal attention to taste and comfort. The drawing room, with its two deep window-recesses, struck me as enormously cheerful. . . . In the room itself sparkled a cheerful fire; choice pictures adorned the walls, and several sofas of various forms, tables covered with curiosities, and furniture standing about in agreeable disorder, gave it the most inviting and home-like air."

It looks as if the windows originally had valances to the curtains, for the cornice is shown over the right-hand window, but this arrangement had been changed to curtains hung on rings from a sturdy pole of wood or brass. The watercolour seems to have been done in summertime because of the way the sofa is placed with its back to the fire facing the inevitable circular centre table. The banquettes facing each other in the recess on the left are of a type seldom seen today.

63
THE DRAWING ROOM AT GUY'S CLIFFE, WARWICKSHIRE. *An anonymous watercolour, about 1860.*

Sledmere, Yorkshire

Today the interior of Sledmere is a splendid restoration after a fire in 1911, but many of the original designs survive and they show how Sir Christopher Sykes, the second baronet, who inherited in 1783, developed his own scheme for enlarging the existing house, using some of the ideas in Samuel Wyatt's plans. Between Sir Christopher's books of drawings and Walter Brierley's restoration come Thomas Malton's view of the Library and amateur watercolours done in 1847. Malton's watercolour, in the context of this book, is of particular interest because it illustrates the neo-classical approach: it was essentially architect-dominated with furniture and figures being merely incidental. Sixty years later the approach was quite different, as the 1847 drawings show. The great feature of the Drawing Room was its fine ceiling by Joseph Rose, who was closely involved with Sir Christopher, and this was skilfully restored after the fire. The pictures and furniture, however, survived, and the same set of chairs and settees is still in the room. Their completely formal disposition round the walls as late as 1847 is rather surprising, but there had to be some compromise with chairs brought up to the centre table, and the sewing tables must have been moved at will. The big portrait on the end wall, painted about 1810, is of Sir Mark Masterman Sykes, the third baronet, his second wife, Elizabeth Egerton of Tatton, and his younger brother, Tatton, who succeeded in 1823 and was forced to sell Sir Mark's library.

64
THE LIBRARY AT SLEDMERE, YORKSHIRE. *A watercolour by Thomas Malton, about 1790.*

Much of it was bought by Sir John Thorold of Syston (plate 87).

In the Dining Room Sir Christopher Sykes may have decided to keep the ceiling of the old house, and for the walls chose 'but few ornaments, rather in the old style . . . as suiting to a plain country gentleman', which was his avowed aim. At the far end of the room can be seen Romney's full-length portrait of Sir Christopher and his wife. Presumably the big table in the centre could have been extended by adding on the folding tables standing beneath the pier glasses, where permanent pier tables would have been expected in the late 18th century. This mobility is also seen in the two pairs of fire screens, one pair behind chairs, hunting chairs with their back cushions pulled up and a pair of armchairs facing each other. This arrangement suggests a scene like that of breakfast at Petworth (Plate 21).

65 and 66
THE DINING ROOM AND DRAWING ROOM. *Anonymous watercolours, about 1847.*

Elton Hall, Huntingdonshire

THE DRAWING ROOM

67
THE LIBRARY AT ELTON HALL, HUNTINGDON. *A watercolour by Capt William Wells, 1818.*

Captain William Wells RN, who was married to the youngest daughter of the house, seems to have had the equivalent of a wide-angle lens in 1818 when he did a watercolour, now varnished, of the principal room in the ancient house, and it seems more than likely that he had experience of drawing for naval purposes. The room, formed partly out of the 16th-century chapel, had been decorated about 1750–60 by the predecessor of the First Earl of Carysfort, who served as ambassador to St Petersburg and Berlin. It is the Earl's four daughters who are shown in the picture, seated round a table in front of the fire, their chairs, like the sofas flanking the fireplace, having case covers bordered with a deep Greek key design that could be seen as a concession to Thomas Hope's influence and recalls the borders to the curtains in the Gallery at Castle Howard (Plate 27). The curtains must have drawn up on cords so as to reveal the shape of the Gothick windows. About 1860 considerable changes were made to the room, so that it would become an appropriate setting for the English and European pictures and French furniture that still remain there.

Stratfield Saye
Hampshire

THE LIBRARY

It is rare that visual evidence about changing taste in one generation survives, and so the existence of both the Duchess of Wellington's drawing of the Library in 1821 and Robert Thorburn's miniature of the Great Duke with his grandchildren completed in 1853 after the Duke's death is particularly fortunate. When the Duke bought Stratfield Saye, he had planned to replace the 17th- and 18th-century house, but he had taken over a certain amount of furniture from the Second Lord Rivers. According to an inventory some curtains were included, including the Library's 'handsome buff and black super fine cotton drapery . . . lin'd with yellow callico . . . [with] gilt and Japann'd cornice with bronze lion heads'. Some changes to the early neo-classical room originally fitted up by George Pitt, the First Lord Rivers, were made in 1822, and in 1838 the elaborate Regency curtains were replaced by much simpler blue striped ones, the same material being used for wall hangings and upholstery as can be seen in the minia-

ture. Thorburn also shows the wall behind the screen of columns taken down to link the Library and Billiard Room. The posing of the children is not entirely fanciful because the boy in the picture, Henry, later the Third Duke, remembered how he and his sisters were given the envelopes from the morning's post to play with in the library.

68 and 69
THE LIBRARY AT STRATFIELD SAYE, HAMPSHIRE. *A drawing by the Duchess of Wellington in 1821 and Robert Thorburn's commemorative miniature of the Great Duke and his grandchildren painted in 1853.*

Renishaw Hall
Derbyshire

The drawings of Renishaw show it in the time of Sir George Sitwell, the second baronet, who had succeeded his father, Sir Sitwell Sitwell, in 1811. The latter, who had inherited in 1793 and had been made a baronet in 1808, had employed Joseph Badger of Sheffield to enlarge the Jacobean house. First the Dining Room was built, between 1793 and 1795; then the Drawing Room was added on, and, after it was completed in 1803, a start was made on the Ballroom, which was finished in time for the Prince Regent's visit in 1806. Apart from the watercolour of the Drawing Room about 1820 by Sewell, the views were done from memory by Georgiana Caroline Sitwell, Mrs Campbell Swinton, when she stayed at Renishaw in the winter of 1853 several years after the sale of the contents.

The Oak Parlour had evidently been the library-cum-living room of the family, and in the overmantel appears Perugino's *The Three Maries*, acquired by Sir Sitwell and sold to the Metropolitan Museum, New York, by Sir George, the fourth baronet, in 1903. Otherwise the room looks much the same today. The Little Parlour, on the other hand, has been simplified, and all that survives is the pattern of the original beams with the rose and the niche between the windows. The appearance of the unusual blind painted to look like stained glass – apparently the only one known – suggests that the walls may have been painted, papered or panelled in a related Gothick style. The elaborately turned armed chair has always belonged to the Sitwells and is still at Renishaw.

The Dining Room is one of Badger's rooms and was originally painted a pink colour that is not apparent in the watercolour. The carved table in the apse with its atlantes legs was sold in 1847, but part of it was recovered and restored by Sir Osbert Sitwell; the colza oil lamp has gone from the niche, but there is still a screen hiding the door leading towards the kitchen.

Although, according to contemporaries,

Sir Sitwell Sitwell had furnished the house with great extravagance, only a few objects, apart from the family pictures and old oak furniture, survived the sale of 1847. Among them is the celebrated Chippendale commode that still stands between the two doors on the west wall of the Drawing Room beneath the Sargent painting of Sir George and Lady Ida Sitwell and their family, painted for that position. One panel from the set of tapestries by de Vos appears in Sewell's picture – there are now three in the room – and corners of the two settees supplied by Thomas Oxenham of Oxford Street in 1808. They are still in the room, as is the massive colza oil chandelier. The room shown as the Billiard Room was remodelled for Sir George Sitwell by Edwin Lutyens.

In *Two Generations* Sir Osbert published the reminiscences of Mrs Campbell Swinton and they gave a vivid picture of life at Renishaw in the second baronet's time.

At Renishaw the hours of meals were rather later than at most other country houses. Breakfast from 1826 to 1846 was nominally at ten, but often did not begin until eleven o'clock. In the year last named, luncheon was at two, and in 1834 dinner at half-past six, though in Derbyshire six o'clock seems to have been more usual. An English breakfast comprised only tea and toast, with an egg for the elder people if they desired it.... But to those, who like my mother, were used to the profusion of a Scottish breakfast, toast was not enough, and something had to be added. In 1826, as a friend remembered, mutton cutlets were served at Renishaw every morning.... In 1840 the meal had been more substantial, there being large pieces of brawn, ham, cold meat and game, as well as quantities of jam, upon the table and sideboard. ... It was not until about 1849 or 1850, when I was about twenty-six or twenty-seven, that five o'clock tea in the drawing room was made an institution, and then only in a few fashionable houses where the dinner was as late as half-past seven or eight o'clock. ...

71 and 72
THE OAK PARLOUR AND DINING ROOM.
Plates 71–74 are watercolours done from memory in 1853 by Mrs Campbell Swinton.

70
THE DRAWING ROOM AT RENISHAW HALL, DERBYSHIRE. *A watercolour by Sewell, about 1820.*

Capesthorne Hall Cheshire

Capesthorne as it exists today is largely a restoration by Salvin after a fire in 1861, but the design owes much to Blore's remodelling of the 18th-century house in the late 1830s. A guidebook produced between 1847 and 1853 under the title *A Whitsuntide Ramble to Capesthorne Park* says: 'The style of the architecture is said to be early English . . .' which is a fair enough description of the transformation carried out for Edward Davies Davenport as soon as he inherited in 1837. Perhaps it was intended to suggest his ancestors' long connection with the estate, but unlike his forbears E. D. Davenport was a Radical, not a Tory, the friend of Harriet Martineau, Francis Burdett, Sydney Smith and Richard Cobden. A great traveller in the classical world, he collected sculpture, Etruscan antiquities and vases as well as fine books.

Fortunately most of his collections survived the fire and many of his acquisitions still at Capesthorne can be recognized in a series of watercolours of the house done by James Johnson of Macclesfield, who was a joiner employed on the remodelling of the house for Blore. Despite the external symmetry of the composition, Blore altered the plan so that the main entrance was, and still is, not in the centre of the east front but within the arch to the stable court beside the north-east tower. This led to a corridor-cum-hall, the first part serving also as a Billiard Room, and leading straight ahead into the Drawing Room facing north. Left out of the hall lay the Sculpture Gallery, which passed the Dining Room before reaching the main staircase. South of the Drawing Room were the ante-room and two more Drawing Rooms

◁

73 and 74
THE LITTLE PARLOUR AND THE BILLIARD ROOM AT RENISHAW.

75 and 76
THE ENTRANCE CORRIDOR AND THE DRAWING ROOM AT CAPESTHORNE HALL, CHESHIRE. *Plates 75–80 are watercolours by James Johnson, about 1840.*

that E. D. Davenport fitted out as Libraries; and beyond them the Conservatory and at the far end the Chapel. The old entrance hall also became a Library. The sequence of rooms is important, because Salvin rearranged the plan.

The style of Blore's Hall may have been Old English, with its stained glass set by Willement in its upper lights and its oak panelling and shutters, but it was modern in what appears to be a gas light over the billiard table. Minor changes have been made since the 1840s, but fortunately the room seems to have survived the fire. When Salvin re-did the Dining Room, he did not repeat the scagliola floor nor the recesses either side of the big window, with casts of statues shaded by crimson draperies.

Although it is undocumented, the centre of the house must have been redecorated about 1780 in the Wyatt style, and Blore retained the neo-classical cornices and ceilings in the three Libraries. E. D. Davenport, his wife and son appear in the view of the East Library, and round the top of the shelves can be seen some of his collection of Etruscan votive heads. There were more in the West Library, where they were mixed with bronzes. Of this room the guidebook said, 'Now this is just such a room as vindicates for English social life, the exclusive use of the word "comfortable"'. Although the family were at home, all the seat furniture is shown carefully protected by its case covers, and apparently there were no flowers, except, of course, in the great Conservatory, which was probably designed by Paxton about 1838. It was influenced by the Great Stove at Chatsworth, built to his design in 1836–40. The columns and main beams were of iron, the curved beams of wood, and the roof itself of a ridge-and-furrow type like the Great Stove. The Conservatory was used as a reception room and also for the Sunday School, the guidebook referring to the 'Precious truths of scripture taught amidst the fitting sights and scenes of flowers'.

Of 18th-century Capesthorne all that is visible today is the Chapel built by Francis Smith of Warwick in 1722, and so it is appropriate that one of the watercolours should be of the family pew during a service, with the preacher in his centrally-placed pulpit.

Tatton Park, Cheshire

THE LIBRARY

Lady Belgrave wrote: 'I always like being at Tatton, the Egertons are always so very kind and fond of us and the house is so pleasant and handsome and gentleman like with every comfort, bodily and mental, of chairs, sofas, books etc. . . .' She was writing of the house in the time of Wilbraham Egerton, who had succeeded his father in 1806 and was married to a Sykes of Sledmere. It was he who called in Lewis Wyatt in 1809 to complete the house originally designed for his father by Samuel Wyatt. Buckler's watercolour of the library in 1820 shows it as it was finished about 1811 with the arrival of the Gillow bookcases and chairs. Gillow probably supplied the circular table hidden by a cloth in the Buckler watercolour and still in the room. The big bookcases and 'commode' bookcases between the windows are still there, but the original pier glasses have gone; also the ceiling and frieze have been altered and there is no longer a continued drapery at the windows.

81

THE LIBRARY AT TATTON PARK, CHESHIRE. *A watercolour by John Buckler, 1820.*

Stourhead, Wiltshire

'I believe there is not a library in the Kingdom so well supplied' with books on British history and topography, wrote the Rev John Skinner in 1824, and he continued: 'Sir Richard can put his hand on the minutest book at a moments notice.' The original books have gone and so have the Canalettos flanking the chimneypiece in Francis Nicholson's watercolour of 1813, and the chimneypiece itself has been changed, but in almost every other way this great room remains as Sir Richard Colt Hoare created it between 1793 and 1805. Having been left a widower in 1785 after only two years of marriage, he travelled abroad for six years, and when he returned to Stourhead he decided to add a Library and a Picture Gallery as flanking wings to the original Palladian house. The shell of the Library was complete about 1795, but the bookcases were not made until 1801, the stained glass not until 1804, and the big library table, the last and finest piece of the younger Thomas Chippendale's furniture, was not delivered until 1805. The present carpet is a copy of the original Wilton whose design is based on a Roman pavement.

Two other interior drawings exist, by John Buckler, of the Saloon and the Little Dining Room. Both rooms were destroyed when the centre block was gutted by fire in 1902, and, while the restored Saloon was drastically redesigned, the Little Dining Room was only modified. However, the alteration meant that it was no longer practical to place Chippendale's sideboard of 1802, which supports the gilt dish presented to Richard Hoare when Lord Mayor of London in 1745, behind the screen of columns, and the statues no longer stand in the end bays. On the other hand the close hanging of the mainly small pictures has been retained, and thus the room acts as a kind of cabinet room to the Gallery.

82

THE LIBRARY AT STOURHEAD, WILTSHIRE. *A watercolour by Francis Nicholson, 1813.*

83

THE LITTLE DINING ROOM. *A watercolour by John Buckler.*

Wrest Park, Bedfordshire

Just as it is rare to find more than one 19th-century view of a room, it is rare to find records of a room in an old house and of its successor in the new one. For Wrest, however, there is a drawing by John Buckler of the old Library, and a watercolour by Thomas Scandrett of the new one. Buckler, who must have done his drawing before the Second Earl de Grey succeeded his aunt in 1833, shows a room with a fine Charles II ceiling, which suggests that it was one of the rooms constructed by the Eleventh Earl of Kent in the 1670s in the house engraved by Kip. It looks as if the rest of the room had been remodelled by the Duke of Kent, a great patron of architects between 1702 and his death in 1740, and remembered for his employment of Archer, Leoni, Hawksmoor and Kent. Here the detail looks more Gibbsian. Among the details of upholstery perhaps the most striking is that of the portière with its valance.

Lord de Grey, who had begun to make architectural changes at Wrest as early as 1816 and had made a special study of 18th-century French architecture and decoration in the late 1820s, felt that 'A *new* house appeared to be indispensable if the place was to be retained as a family Residence, which, with so large a county property and consequent county influences, was a matter of necessity.' He began the new house in 1834 and completed it five years later, being responsible not only for the design but for the details. Half the state rooms were allotted to Libraries of which there were three, and the

84
THE LIBRARY IN THE OLD HOUSE A WREST PARK, BEDFORDSHIRE. *A drawi by John Buckler.*

one illustrated led out of the staircase ha with the entrance hall beyond. Despite Lor de Grey's careful study of 18th-centur books and engravings, the detail of this roor looks typical of the Louis Revival of th 1830s, with its cast and rather coarsel modelled ornament.

85 and 86
ONE OF THE LIBRARIES AND TI TAPESTRY DRAWING ROOM IN THE NE HOUSE. *Watercolours by Thomas Scandrett.*

Syston, Lincolnshire

In the third decade of the 19th century the design of country houses and clubs had a great influence on each other, and, if the inscription to the view of the Syston Library had been lost, only the figure of the lady would suggest that the room was in the country and not overlooking gardens behind Pall Mall. The centre part of Syston had been built for Sir John Thorold, the ninth baronet, who succeeded in 1775 and died in 1815, by John Langwith, and in 1824 Sir John-Harford Thorold, the tenth baronet, added on both the Library and the Conservatory designed by Vulliamy. Sir John-Harford Thorold was a great book collector and made many purchases at the Sledmere sale, and it is this that explains the great size of the top lit room, 60 × 31 feet, with a gallery. Much of the furniture was supplied by Gillows. The Conservatory was equally ambitious.

87
THE LIBRARY AT SYSTON, LINCOLN-
SHIRE. An engraving after T. Kearman.

88
THE CONSERVATORY. *An engraving prob-
ably based on a drawing by the architect Lewis
Vulliamy.*

THE BILLIARD ROOM AT LISMORE
CASTLE, IRELAND. *An anonymous watercolour, about 1825.*

THE BILLIARD ROOM AT BEAUFRONT
CASTLE, NORTHUMBERLAND. *A watercolour probably by the architect John Dobson,
with figures by J. W. Carmichael.*

Lismore Castle
Co. Waterford, Eire
and
Beaufront Castle
Northumberland

THE BILLIARD ROOMS

The Victorians devoted great thought to
billiard rooms, both to their placing and
fitting up, and these two illustrations show
very different solutions. Robert Kerr, for
instance, wrote in *The Gentleman's House*
(1864): 'The position of a Billiard room is
probably best when it opens either from a
large Entrance Hall or from the entrance end
of the Principal corridor or Gallery, and so as
to be situated not exactly amongst the
Dwelling rooms, but still in close communi-

cation with them. Sometimes it is placed as an
external appendage, approached by a short
balcony or covered way; but this is for smok-
ing.' At Lismore the Sixth Duke of Devonshire placed the table in the hall, in the first
part of the house to be altered for him by
William Atkinson between 1812 and 1822.
Kerr would not have approved, particularly
in the house of such an important person, but
the Duke was much less self-conscious and
Lismore was primarily a house for holidays,
relaxed and informal, as can be seen from the
hats and coats lying carelessly on the side
table. The billiard table was lit by a set of colza
oil lamps mounted in a frame.

The Beaufront Billiard Room was a much
more elaborate affair, and evidently the
architect of the house, John Dobson, was
very proud of it, as he was of the whole house.
Presumably it was he who did the architectural perspective and got J. W. Carmichael, a
local artist, to add the figures of the Cuthbert

family with one of him showing his plans for
the house, begun in 1837. Its baronial character with armour, flags and horns was unusual,
but Kerr would have surely approved of the
arrangements: 'This apartment in ordinary
cases is not meant to withstand the criticism
of players; and therefore when it is, it must be
rather more fastidiously planned than is nor-
mal. The difficulty lies more particularly in
the arrangement of lights. . . .' He was keen
on overhead lighting of the kind provided by
Dobson, and he also recommended 'fixed
benches or couches along part of the walls,
elevated a few inches by a banquette or step'.
Rather ecclesiastical-looking benches were
acquired for Beaufront, and players sitting on
the one on the right could have warmed their
toes on the heating grating that ran in front of
it. Unfortunately virtually all the fittings and
Gillows' furniture have gone, but the room
itself survives, the most remarkable interior
in Dobson's favourite house.

Scone Palace, Perthshire

THE GALLERY

In 1803 the Third Earl of Mansfield began rebuilding Scone to the design of William Atkinson, a task that took nine years. The Long Gallery had been an exceptional feature of the earlier house on the site, and Atkinson's replacement, 168 feet long, was apparently inspired by Wyatt's cloisters at Wilton. The picture of it by J. Gibb, an obscure Edinburgh painter, which was exhibited at the Royal Academy in 1827, is an unusually detailed record of the room. Many of the objects depicted are still in the Gallery, among them the organ built by Elliott in Edinburgh in 1813, the busts and marbles, and the Gothick centre table. The simple curtains without valances and the upholstery of the chairs and the ottoman were of a heavy crimson woollen material with blue velvet ribbon and cord. The gilt console table on the right looks as if it was probably brought from Kenwood, the First Earl's house, and the gilt chairs covered in needlework are by Pierre Bara. They are now in the Drawing Room, and form part of one of the finest collections of French furniture in Britain.

92 and 93

THE DRAWING ROOM AND LIBRARY A BIGNOR PARK, SUSSEX. *Watercolours a tributed to Thomas Hardwick the Elder.*

Bignor Park, Sussex

John Hawkins acquired Bignor in 1806, but it was not until 1826 that he began the new house to the design of Henry Harrison. By inclination an antiquary, and also interested in geology, science and literature, he had travelled widely in the Near East and Greece, and for his house he chose a sober neoclassical style that was also appropriate for a place made famous by the discovery of the site of a Roman villa. The house was completed in 1831, and John Hawkins died ten years later. Since then Bignor has been little altered and the Dining Room still retains its original furniture. Other pieces are now at Trewithen, in Cornwall, then the seat of the senior branch of the Hawkins family and still in the possession of John Hawkins's descendants. Now reunited with them there are these two unusually confident and well set-out watercolours of the Drawing Room and Library at Bignor, apparently by the elder Thomas Hardwicke who was drawing master to the young Miss Hawkins. One of the young ladies appears in the unfinished watercolour of the Drawing Room, surrounded by some of her father's pictures. The details are particularly clear, the use of stepped rods for the pictures, for instance, the domes on many of the ornaments and careful cutting of the pattern of the material used for the cover of the sofa. It does not appear to have been a very formal room, but the Library next door looks as if it was the everyday living-room with its mixture of chairs round the centre table, each member of the family probably choosing one to suit their own needs, with little concern for the visual effect. This informality contrasts with the architectural design of the room, with its spare plaster detail, its yellow scagliola pilasters and the acroteria on the bookcase.

Somerley, Hampshire

THE PICTURE GALLERY

The Second Earl of Normanton, who designed and built the gallery about 1850, had begun to collect pictures about 1816, some twelve years before he bought Somerley. Like several of his contemporaries he greatly admired Reynolds and acquired no fewer than twenty-seven pictures by him. Many of these can be identified in the two pictures painted for him by C. J. Walker in 1853 at the cost of £9 12s the pair. Gustav Waagen, the celebrated chronicler of English collections, who visited Somerley in 1854, was very impressed.

But my Chief Pleasure and surprise was the stately picture gallery. . . . The proportions are not only fine, and the gold decorations rich and tasteful, but the lighting from above is so happily calculated that every picture receives a clean and gentle light, while the reflections which so much disturb the enjoyment of the similarly lighted Bridgewater Gallery are quite avoided. This end is attained more especially by the fact that the light falls only from each side of the roof, the whole length of the centre being kept dark. . . .

At night, as in the Waterloo Gallery at Apsley House, the windows are hidden by great plates of mirror glass. Some changes in the hanging of the pictures have taken place over the years, but the collection is one of the few of the period to remain more or less intact.

94 and 95
THE PICTURE GALLERY AT SOMERLEY, HAMPSHIRE. *Paintings by C. J. Walker, 1853.*

6 and 97
THE DINING ROOM AND PICTURE
GALLERY AT ATTINGHAM PARK,
SHROPSHIRE. *Watercolours by Lady Hester
Leeke.*

Attingham Park
Shropshire

Lady Hester Leeke, who lived at Longford,
near Newport, painted watercolours of many
Shropshire houses, and among those of particular interest are two of Attingham showing
the Dining Room and Picture Gallery. The
house then belonged to the Fifth Lord Berwick, who succeeded in 1848 and died in
1861. George Steuart's elegant Dining
Room, fitted up for the First Lord Berwick in
the late 1780s, had been painted a Pompeian
red when Nash altered the house for the Second Lord Berwick about 1805. In recent
years it has been impossible to judge the full
effect of the room because of its use, but Lady
Hester shows the table laid for dinner, with
the handsome Gillow chairs drawn up and
what appear to be pieces of French ormolu set
down the table. The chairs were bought in at
the 1827 sale of the contents of the house,
and so evidently was the continued drapery,
which presumably dated from about 1805. In
the watercolour it looks blue, but the sale
catalogue described the curtains as

the splendid suite of four pair of fine drab cloth
French rod window curtains, handsomely bordered with four inch Purple Velvet, and two rows
of rich Gold-colour Silk Lace, Elegant deep Cloth
and Velvet Drapery, continued over the piers, and

tastefully displayed in Festoons, bordered *en suite*,
and trimmed with Gold-colour Silk, and Worsted
Parisian Fringe, supported by thick twisted Ropes,
and large Turkish Tassels.

Even then they cost £89 5s, and the brown
holland covering for the drapery cost another
£1 1s. As well as the side table at the end of
the room there is a serving table on the
fireplace wall, and its curtain is the same colour as the upholstery.

Nash formed the Picture Gallery to take
the collection formed by the Second Baron
chiefly in Italy in the 1790s. Most of the best
pictures were sold in 1827, but sufficient

were bought in to create an impressive effect
on the glossy Chinese vermilion walls and
they remain *in situ* today, as does all the
furniture shown in the watercolour. Some of
the tables were part of the original furniture
of the Gallery, but all the Italian furniture,
which is an unusual feature of the house, was
acquired by the Third Lord Berwick when he
was in Italy. The plain carpet has a border and
fits within the legs of the tables; round it is a
fine parquet border laid when the room was
formed. The watercolours confirm how little
the room has changed since the mid-19th
century.

98
THE CONSERVATORY
AT BLITHFIELD HALL,
STAFFORDSHIRE. *A
watercolour by Charlotte-
Anne Sneyd, 1852.*

99
THE CONSERVATORY
AT CUFFNELLS, HAMP-
SHIRE. *A watercolour
by Maria Lushington
(d. 1855).*

Blithfield Hall
Staffordshire

THE SECOND LORD BAGOT IN HIS STUDY
AT BLITHFIELD. *A watercolour by
Charlotte-Anne Sneyd in 1854.*

Cuffnells, Hampshire

THE CONSERVATORY

George Rose (1744–1818) started life as a
sailor but later became a politician, holding
minor office on numerous occasions and
eventually declining the post of Chancellor of
the Exchequer in 1809. He acquired the
house near Lyndhurst about 1785 and in
1794 he employed Soane to make considerable alterations and additions, including the
nine-bay Conservatory with its wooden columns. In 1805 it was described as 'being filled
with a choice assemblage of indigenous and
exotic plants, and, from its size and construction is much admired. It communicates, by
large folding doors, with the library. . . .' On
several occasions George III visited the
house on his journeys to Weymouth. The
watercolour is by Maria Lushington, the
eldest daughter of Sir Henry Lushington, and
was executed in 1847 by which time the
house belonged to the Hargreaves family.
Loudon approved of the idea of placing a
billiard table close to a Conservatory. The
Hargreaves continued to own Cuffnells until
after 1929 and the house was demolished in
1951.

Charlotte Anne Sneyd's watercolour of the
Second Lord Bagot at work in the Oak Room
at Blithfield in 1854 is a delightful record of
an elderly squire of antiquarian leanings.
Having succeeded in 1798, Lord Bagot
recased the ancient house in Gothick dress,
possibly with the aid of John Buckler, who
illustrated Lord Bagot's *Memorials of the Bagot
Family*, which was printed in the newly completed house in 1824. In that book he wrote:
'The rooms are low, irregular and extraordinary; but from their all opening into each
other, and being capable of containing a great
number of people, their irregularity becomes
interesting, and their extraordinary shapes
create a sort of comfort which is frequently
sought for in vain in more magnificent
abodes.' Certainly this is the impression given
by the watercolour of the Conservatory with
Eleanor Bagot, the Second Lord Bagot's
daughter, seated with her dog Trip. The
stained glass has gone from the upper lights of
the bay window, which projects from the
west side of the house, but the marble vase
and pillar are still there, and the room still has
the charming indoors-outdoors character it
had in 1852. The Oak Room, with its
18th-century panelling, had evidently
changed very little during Lord Bagot's
lifetime: it still possessed festoon curtains and
what appear to be prints on the end wall are

hung very high by modern standards, and it
was comfortably full. Lord Bagot could easily
turn to the davenport on his right from the
writing table; or could rest on the chaise-
longue with its deep cushions and cane ends.
Anne Bagot's impression of him in 1833 was
very similar: then she found him 'sitting snug
in the ci-devant pillar'd parlour emblazoning
Newton's book of the British Squires'.

York Buildings, London

SAMUEL PEPYS'S LIBRARY

These are the earliest known accurate records of an identified English interior. Attributed to Sutton Nicholls (fl. about 1700–40), a draughtsman and engraver recorded by Vertue, they were executed as the frontispieces to the two volumes of the MS catalogue of Pepys's library, prepared in 1693. Pepys had moved the Admiralty Office from Derby House to York Buildings in September 1684, and he continued to use the latter, even after his loss of office, until 1700. The main feature of the room was the set of seven bookcases, of which the first two were made for him in 1666 by Thomas Simpson, master-joiner at the Woolwich and Deptford dockyards. Eventually he ended up with twelve and they are now all at Magdalene College, Cambridge. From the beginning the books within them were arranged according to height rather than subject matter, with the leather-faced base blocks specially made to achieve uniformity of height. Over the bolection-moulded fireplace a portrait of James II by Kneller hung flat, while the smaller portraits over the bookcases tipped forward; but there were no overdoors. Nor was there a carpet or mat on the wide-boarded floor, but there were single draw curtains to each window. The writing-table was covered with a fitted cover and the broad chair with its slightly curved back filled with canework was probably made about the same time as the bookcase. Between the windows over a table hung a mirror with elaborate cresting and glass borders ornamented with plaquettes, a piece possibly acquired not long before the drawings were done. The presence of the large map hung from books is reminiscent of details in pictures of Dutch interiors. Through the open door an early folding card table can be seen.

101 and 102
SAMUEL PEPYS'S LIBRARY AT YORK
BUILDINGS, LONDON. *Drawings attributed to Sutton Nicholls, 1693.*

Grosvenor House, London

THE GALLERY

Few pictures convey so vividly the opulent confidence of the richest aristocratic families in the post-Waterloo period as C. R. Leslie's *Grosvenor Family*, painted in 1831 to celebrate the creation of the Marquessate of Westminster. Lord Westminster, the former Second Earl Grosvenor and builder of Eaton Hall, is seated in the centre with his grandson, Hugh Lupus, later the First Duke of Westminster; his elder son and heir Lord Belgrave, later the Second Marquess, stands behind him, and Lady Westminster is seated at the piano. Their youngest son, Lord Robert, later created Lord Ebury, is on the left, and next to him Lady Belgrave, who found Eaton so comfortless and Tatton so agreeable; on the right is the middle son, Lord Wilton, with his wife. They are shown in the Gallery recently extended by the Cundys to take the four vast canvases by Rubens bought in 1818, which appear behind the columns.

Lord Grosvenor had acquired the house in Mayfair in 1805, changing its name from Gloucester to Grosvenor, and the Gallery had been added on at that time by Porden to take the very fine collection that had been formed by Lord Grosvenor and his father. Like several contemporary collections it was concentrated in London, and virtually nothing then thought to be of importance was sent to Eaton. Among the pictures identifiable and still in the collection is Velasquez's *Don Carlos on Horseback*, which can be seen behind Lord Wilton's head.

When the Gallery was extended, Lord

103

THE GROSVENOR FAMILY. *C. R. Leslie's picture showing the Gallery at Grosvenor House, London in 1831.*

Grosvenor had contemplated a complete remodelling and vast extension of the house that would have made it as grand as Stafford House was to be, but the plans were abandoned. In 1872–3 the Gallery was altered once more and after the sale of the house in 1924 it was demolished to make way for the hotel in Park Lane that bears its name today.

104 and 105
THE DUKE OF WELLINGTON'S BEDROOM
AND STUDY AT APSLEY HOUSE, LONDON.
Plates 104–107 are from Richard Ford's Apsley
House and Walmer Castle *(1852).*

106 and 107
THE STRIPED DRAWING ROOM AND THE
GALLERY SET OUT FOR A WATERLOO
DINNER.

Apsley House, London

Shortly after the Great Duke of Wellington's death in 1852 Richard Ford published a tribute to him in the form of a folio book, *Apsley House and Walmer Castle*, illustrated with coloured lithographs. The views of the London house are particularly interesting because of the way they emphasize the contrast between the splendour of the public rooms and the modesty, indeed the austerity, of the Duke's own apartments. In part this contrast was accidental, for the alterations and additions were made by the Duke in a piecemeal fashion, but in the end his friend Mrs Arbuthnot tried to persuade him to see it as his 'Waterloo House'.

Richard Ford called The Striped Drawing Room the 'Walhalla' as it was filled with the portraits of the Duke's family, 'the comrades of his arms', the striped hangings and upholstery giving it a slightly earlier Regency character than is suggested by Benjamin Wyatt's amalgamation of his own and the original Adam detail, the crispness of line even recalling the tent decorations of the early Empire.

The climax to the house was the Waterloo Gallery begun in 1828, partly to house the large pictures that the Duke had acquired and also to provide a larger room for banquets on the anniversary of the battle, of which the first was held in 1830. Benjamin Wyatt's lack of control over the costs led to great bitterness, and the Duke left the final stages of the room

to Mrs Arbuthnot, but it was he who insisted on yellow for the damask hangings, a colour that both she and Wyatt thought would be disastrous. 'Yellow hangings will entirely destroy the effect of the gilding in the room,' wrote Wyatt, 'any colour that shall be in contrast with the gold will give it its full effect but yellow, I assure Your grace, will sadly diminish it.' The table is shown with the great Russian porphyry torchères rising through from the floor, and in the centre can be seen the Portuguese service made in 1816. Despite Wyatt's unsatisfactory conduct, Mrs Arbuthnot was rightly pleased with the result, for it is among the grandest rooms in London and a splendid justification for the architect's development of the Louis Revival in England.

108

THE STAIRCASE AT STAFFORD HOUSE, LONDON. *An anonymous watercolour about 1850.*

Stafford House, London

When Thomas Moore went to Stafford House in 1830, before the state rooms were decorated, he thought 'nothing can be more magnificent than the staircase; its size and grandeur made the whole company look both pigmy and dingy. Lady Stafford received the company in a manner worthy of the staircase.' Her husband, the Second Marquess (later First Duke of Sutherland) had taken a lease in 1827 of the unfinished house begun by the Duke of York, and had completed the ground-floor rooms by the end of 1830. However, the rich colouring of the upper walls of the staircase and the addition of the copies after Veronese date from 1840–4 and are probably part of Barry's work for the Second Duke. The watercolourist shows yet again how early Victorians managed to make their larger houses look like clubs and hotels, and there is a strange dichotomy between the informally arranged chairs in chintz covers

and the grandeur of the scale and decoration. Instead it should be seen through the eyes of the formidable Lady Eastlake in 1854:

. . . Buckingham Palace is nothing to it [and Queen Victoria agreed]. The Great Hall and staircases are masters of architecture, fulfilling many conditions of beauty in proportion, design, size and decoration; and, as all places of entertainment should, it attains its full beauty when crowded with figures. Not that there could be any crowd. . . . All was marble, bronze, gilding, pictures, gorgeous hangings and carpets, with flowers without end. No picture by Veronese of a marriage feast can exceed in gorgeousness what was presented to our eye.

The truth of this is to be seen in a plate in the *Illustrated London News* ten years later, showing a reception for Garibaldi, at that time a liberal revolutionary making a trium-

109

THE ASSEMBLY IN HONOUR OF GARIBALDI IN THE GALLERY. *From* The Illustrated London News *(1864).*

phant visit to London, who was taken up by the Third Duke and Duchess. The Gallery had been more or less completed in the mid 1830s for the Second Duke, with final details supervised by Charles Barry when he succeeded B. D. Wyatt. It contained pictures partly inherited from the First Duke, who had been one of those involved in the purchase of the Orleans collection, and partly acquired by the Second Duke and Duchess when they decorated the state rooms.

110
THE WHITE ROOM AT AUBREY HOUSE,
LONDON. *Plates 110–114 are watercolours by
Louisa Goldsmid about 1818.*

111
THE HEAD OF THE STAIRS.

Aubrey House, London

Aubrey House still stands on the heights of Campden Hill, a country house in the heart of Kensington. Now most often associated with Lady Mary Coke, who lived there in the third quarter of the 18th century, and in recent decades with the Alexander family, it was in the early 19th century the home of the de Vismes. Having taken a lease in 1807, P. N. de Visme moved in the following year and died there in 1817, his widow continuing to live in the house until the autumn of 1819. One of their daughters, Louisa, who married John Louis Goldsmid in 1809 when she was twenty-eight, painted a series of watercolours of the exterior dated 1817, and the interior, which give a delightful sense of its clarity and simplicity at that time. In the White Room,

for instance, there was an 18th-century austerity: the chairs, with their neatly nailed seats, were ranged round the walls and set back in the reveals of the windows; there were spring blinds and no curtains, and the floor looks as if it may have been painted to resemble black and white marble squares. The Drawing-Room was richer, with traces of James Wyatt's decoration for Lady Mary Coke in 1774, but evidently elaborated by the de Vismes. It was presumably they who introduced the Regency pier glass, put up the wallpaper with its feigned drapery, and hung the curtains with their valances suspended from the gilded rod. The pots of flowers in the long basket on the stand are a rarely recorded kind of detail. The furniture in both Drawing Room and Dining Room, on the other hand, looks quite simple, and it is interesting to see some of the Dining Room chairs drawn up to the baize-covered table and some set back against the walls. The lives led by children at that time are seldom recorded, and it is exceptional to find not only a drawing of the children playing at the head of the stairs, but another of them with their nurse in the nursery. The chairs in the Sheraton style and with case covers over their seats look as if they started life in a Drawing Room a generation earlier, while it is rare to find a simple bed with a white canopy.

113

THE DRAWING ROOM.

112

THE NURSERY.

114

THE DINING ROOM AND THE GALLERY